# LINCOLNSHIRE

The Reverend Henry Thorold is the author of *Lincolnshire Churches Revisited* (Foreword by H. R. H. The Prince of Wales), *Collins Guide to Cathedrals, Abbeys and Priories*, *Collins Guide to the Ruined Abbeys of England, Wales and Scotland*, and five of the celebrated Shell Guides to the English Counties, including *Nottinghamshire*, which won the 1985 Thomas Cook Award for the best guide book. He was a housemaster at Lancing College for many years. He is a Trustee of the Historic Churches Preservation Trust and Chairman of the Lincolnshire Old Churches Trust. He lives at Marston Hall, near Grantham, a home of the Thorold family since the fourteenth century.

Pimlico County History Guides
(General editor: Christopher Hibbert)

*Already published*:

*Bedfordshire* by Simon Houfe
*Cambridgeshire* by Ross Clark
*Dorset* by Richard Ollard
*Norfolk* by Tom Pocock
*Somerset* (with Bath and Bristol) by Shirley Toulson
*Suffolk* by Miles Jebb
*Sussex* by Desmond Seward

*Forthcoming*:

*Cumbria* by Alan Hankinson
*Oxfordshire* by John Steane

# LINCOLNSHIRE

---

## HENRY THOROLD
### with a Foreword by Christopher Hibbert

A PIMLICO COUNTY HISTORY GUIDE

To Anthony Henry Thorold
15th Baronet of Marston
645th High Sheriff of Lincolnshire
1st Leader of the Lincolnshire County Council

*Haec olim meminisse juvabit*

PIMLICO

An imprint of Random House
20 Vauxhall Bridge Road, London SW1V 2SA

Random House Australia (Pty) Ltd
20 Alfred Street, Milsons Point, Sydney
New South Wales 2061, Australia

Random House New Zealand Ltd
18 Poland Road, Glenfield
Auckland 10, New Zealand

Random House South Africa (Pty) Ltd
PO Box 337, Bergvlei, South Africa

Random House UK Ltd Reg. No. 954009

First published by Pimlico 1996

1 3 5 7 9 10 8 6 4 2

Papers used by Random House UK Limited are natural,
recyclable products made from wood grown in sustainable
forests. The manufacturing processes conform to the
environmental regulations of the country of origin

Typeset by Deltatype Ltd, Ellesmere Port, Cheshire
Printed and bound in Great Britain by
Mackays of Chatham plc, Chatham, Kent

ISBN 0-7126-9892-2

# Contents

# Acknowledgements

It was my old friend Mr Richard Ollard who first suggested that I might write *Lincolnshire* in this series; he had himself written *Dorset*, which was published last year and has already given great pleasure to many readers. I was indeed grateful, but at first uncertain: I already had three Lincolnshire books behind me – what more was there to say? I need not have feared. Lincolnshire never disappoints. There are always new discoveries, new surprises, new ideas. I had much encouragement, much help, from many friends, and must pay tribute to them.

It was Lord and Lady Monson who reminded me of the importance of the Royal Air Force in the history of the county, showed me the pulpit in South Carlton Church and told me of the early days of the Royal Flying Corps there. Mr Bryan Lilley took me on splendid tours of R.A.F. sites in the county, conducting me to places which I should never have discovered by myself. It was Mr David Lawrence MBE who introduced me to the history of the railways in the county, and drove me for miles and miles to the sites of extinct lines, and to survey the surviving lines, railway bridges, stations, signal boxes and signals. What enjoyment they have provided! Mr Peter Dennis told me much about his remarkable grandfather and kindly read Chapter XX before it went to press. Mr Barry Jones very kindly provided me with the details about the Humber Bridge, and Captain Jeremy Elwes DL gave me the facts about that most unfortunate episode: the creation of so-called 'Humberside'. I am indeed grateful to all these friends.

Most grateful thanks, too, to Mr and Mrs Peter Ball, Mr John Barratt, Mr Guy Bedford, Mr Alan Black, the late Mr Peter Brannan, Dr Edward Brown, Dr David Crook, Mr Michael Cyprien, Mr Hugh Goodliffe-Wayman, the Venerable Dr David Griffiths and Mrs Griffiths, Mr and the Hon. Mrs Michael Hodges, Mrs Howard-Leech, Prebendary Gerard Irvine, Mrs Nigel Kerr, Mr Peter Mackenzie, Miss Diana Marvin, Mr Hugh Montgomery-Massingberd, Mr Gordon Partington, Mr and Mrs Robert Rankin, Dr John Martin Robinson, Mr Peter Sanderson and Mr John Stevens-Guille, all of whom helped in important ways. I am much indebted to Mr and Mrs Stuart Losco-Bradley: it was she who typed out the book in record time for the publisher.

As always, abundant thanks to Mr Peter Burton and Mr Harland Walshaw for a wonderful set of new Lincolnshire photographs: their remarkable ingenuity and the originality of their photographs are always refreshing. Great gratitude, too, once again, to Mr and Mrs Karl Ballaam for their unfailing help. Where should I be but for his central heating and her delicious food?

Finally, I must record the pleasure it has been to work with my publisher, Mr Will Sulkin, and my editor, Mr Euan Cameron: I can only thank them for all their help, and their patience.

Henry Thorold
Marston Hall, Grantham
Candlemas, 1996

# Foreword

For those, like me, who know little of Lincolnshire and, indeed, for those who know it far better, Henry Thorold is an ideal guide. His ancient family have lived hereabouts for generation after generation; his own house stands on a property which came into the hands of his forebears by marriage in the fourteenth century. He writes of the county with authority and affection and a kind of proprietorial pride, revealing its out-of-the-way treasures, what he calls its 'surprises', displaying its better known monuments in a fresh light, and writing with a Betjeman-esque nostalgia of the demise of once great houses and of the decline of the old railways; the loss, for example, of 'that enchanting line from Louth through the deepest Wolds to Wragby and Bardney'.

He begins his book by conducting us to several vantage points from which views can be enjoyed over the surrounding countryside – the portico of an ancient church, an eighteenth-century gazebo, the gatehouse of a long-lost abbey, the garden door of a country house – and from such starting points he takes us down to see the villages below. And what wonderfully whimsical names so many of these villages bear: Saltfleetby, Theddlethorpe, Wigtoft, Friskney, Wrangle, Whaplode, Toxt-next-Newton, Silk Willoughby, Stragglethorpe! One is tempted to go on, as with the names of those villages in Dorset whose euphonious syllables so delighted Sir John Betjeman. Their Lincolnshire counterparts sound just like places which might have been invented by Dickens as villages where

Codlin and Short set up their Punch and Judy show in *The Old Curiosity Shop*. In them and elsewhere Mr Thorold immediately seeks out the little known and unexpected. At Monksthorpe he follows a lane marked 'No Through Road' to a small, rectangular gabled building of mellow, plum-coloured brick. It is the oldest Baptist Chapel in Lincoln-shire and one of the oldest in England. Nearby, in the garden, is a small pool with steps leading down to it, a very rare example of an open-air baptismal pond. At Kirkby-cum-Osgodby is the oldest Roman Catholic chapel in Lincolnshire, discreetly disguised so as not to offend the Protestant susceptibilities of King George III. At Croyland is 'one of the greatest curiosities', a fourteenth-century triangular bridge built to take travellers from the three streets of the little town that meet here over the three streams of the River Welland. At Brocklesby, at the end of a long ride in the park, standing in the shade of tall and melancholy cedar trees, is James Wyatt's fine mausoleum built to the memory of the much-loved wife of the first Lord Yarborough whose descendant, the second Earl, raised the nearby Pelham's Pillar which towers above the woodlands near Cabourne to commemorate his planting of twelve million trees. And in towns and villages all over the county are the churches which the author knows so well.

There are hundreds to choose from: in *Collins Guide to Parish Churches* there are more pages devoted to Lincoln-shire than to any other county in England. All the most interesting and beautiful find mention here, from the great, well-known St Wulfram's, Grantham, one of the finest parish churches in England – whose spire Sir George Gilbert Scott considered 'second only to Salisbury in beauty' – and the equally splendid St Botolph's, Boston, to those com-paratively humble, delightful little Fen churches in that part of Lincolnshire known as Holland. Here, indeed, the author believes, is 'the greatest collection anywhere of glorious medieval churches', some with splendid spires 'all pointing

to Heaven', others with lovely towers, Early English at
Whaplode, elegantly Perpendicular at Pinchbeck and Old
Leake, fifteenth-century brick with stone spires at St
Mary's, Tydd St Mary and at Lutton. Four are singled out
for special mention, among them the church of St Mary
Magdalene at Gedney which seems to sail into view, 'almost
transparent with its lofty clerestory of twelve lights, its rows
of traceried windows below'.

Mr Thorold's enthusiasm is infectious. When he tells us
that Stamford is 'the most beautiful of all English towns',
and that Belton is 'the most beautiful of all late seventeenth-
century English houses', we are well on the way to believing
him by the time he has finished describing them. His
necessarily brief description of Lincoln Cathedral, 'one of
the greatest Gothic churches in the world', is not only
persuasive, but as fine and concise an evocation of this
magnificent building as could be wished for.

His affection for his county and admiration for its
buildings is unbounded: Stragglethorpe Church is 'not to be
missed'; St Helen's, Brant Broughton is 'one of the very best
of all Lincolnshire churches'; the gatehouse of Thornton
Abbey 'vies with St Osyth's and Battle for the title of the
grandest monastic gatehouse to survive'; Tattershall is 'that
most magnificent of Tudor castles'; Mrs van der Elst
'should be canonised' for having saved the huge nineteenth-
century Harlaxton Manor, the largest and most extrava-
gant house in Lincolnshire, from demolition.

Yet he is far from undiscriminating in his judgements.
The centre of Grantham has been 'wantonly destroyed'; a
drive through High Street, Watergate or Vine Street is now
'very depressing'; the George, described fifty years ago as
'the best hotel on the Great North Road', has been
converted into a shopping arcade – 'full of empty shops'; a
handsome Georgian house further down the street has been
replaced by a 'barbarous block'. Similar vandalism has been
allowed to take place in Boston where a 'monstrous dual

carriageway makes its slithery way from the Bargate to the Haven Bridge' through the very heart of the ancient town; and in Spalding where the 'appalling monster called the "South Holland Centre" ' has been erected as a blot on the Market Place. Yet cheerfulness keeps breaking in: there is much in Spalding and Boston still to be enjoyed; it is still possible to walk round Grantham without seeing its major horrors. A visit to Sleaford is 'always a pleasure'; Caistor is 'an attractive little town' with 'considerable charm'; Spilsby 'remains enchanting'; there can be 'few fairer towns' to enter than Louth; and a visit to Horncastle 'is also a tonic'.

It is as much a pleasure to be conducted round Lincoln-shire's country houses by such a well-informed enthusiast as it is to be taken through its smaller towns. The author clearly knows them all, and some of them intimately. He is also an expert on the histories of the families who have occupied them and, in several cases, occupy them still. There are grand houses like Grimsthorpe Castle, home of the Willoughby de Eresby family since the early years of the sixteenth century, a house combining the charms of the medieval and Tudor castle with Sir John Vanbrugh's magnificent north front. There are delightful Elizabethan manor houses such as Doddington Hall with its towering façade of old red brick. There are equally enchanting houses in the manner of Fulbeck Hall, home of the Fane family, with a garden of exceptional interest. All these houses are open to the public at certain times of the year, as, indeed, is Henry Thorold's own house, Marston Hall, which also has a lovely garden, although he does not say so.

Gunby Hall at Burgh-le-Marsh, on the other side of the county from Marston Hall, was built by Sir William Massingberd in 1700. It was threatened with demolition during the Second World War so that the runway of a nearby airfield could be extended. The then owner of the house, Field-Marshal Sir Archibald Montgomery-Massingberd appealed to the Secretary of State for Air, then to the Prime Minister without success; but he then approached the King and the house was saved.

This distinguished and resolute old soldier, who had risen from the rank of major to major-general in just over two years, is one of the many intriguing Lincolnshire men and women who make their appearance in the pages of this book, from Isaac Newton, born in the manor house of Woolsthorpe, near Grantham, in 1642, to the actress Joan Plowright born at Scunthorpe in 1929 and educated at the Grammar School there; from St Gilbert of Sempringham, founder of the monastic order which bears his name, to John Wesley, fifteenth child of the Rector of Epworth where he came into the world in 1703 to become the leader of Methodism. Henry IV was born in his father's castle of Bolingbroke, near Spilsby. William Robertson, who rose from the ranks to become a field-marshal, was the son of a villager of Welbourn; Alfred, Lord Tennyson was the fourth of the twelve children of the Rector of Somersby. William of Waynflete, the founder of Magdalen College, Oxford, came from a little place by the shore of the Wash; Thomas Sutton, who had made a fortune by leasing lands rich in coal and who founded Charterhouse School, was born at Knaith.

Another rich and far less renowned Lincolnshire-born entrepreneur was William Dennis, the son of a farm foreman, who came to Kirton in 1861 with a scythe, sickle and rake, to make his fortune. How he did so – out of potatoes of all things – and how he became a 'great son of Lincolnshire' is the theme of the last chapter of this book.

Not far from Horsington, where William Dennis was born, on the other side of Horncastle, is the little village of Langton, home for centuries of the Langtons, one of the oldest Lincolnshire families. Bennet Langton, who was born in 1737, was a close friend of Samuel Johnson; and, as Henry Thorold says, it is pleasant to think of the two men worshipping here in the early eighteenth-century parish church of St Peter and St Paul which, with its tiered seats, three-decker pulpit and gallery, is much the same now as it was then. One can, indeed, picture the two men here: young Langton, tall, thin, long-faced and elegant; Dr Johnson, almost thirty years his senior, clumsy and shambling, wearing an ill-fitting wig, rolling about compulsively as he says his prayers with loud and desperate fervour.

CHRISTOPHER HIBBERT

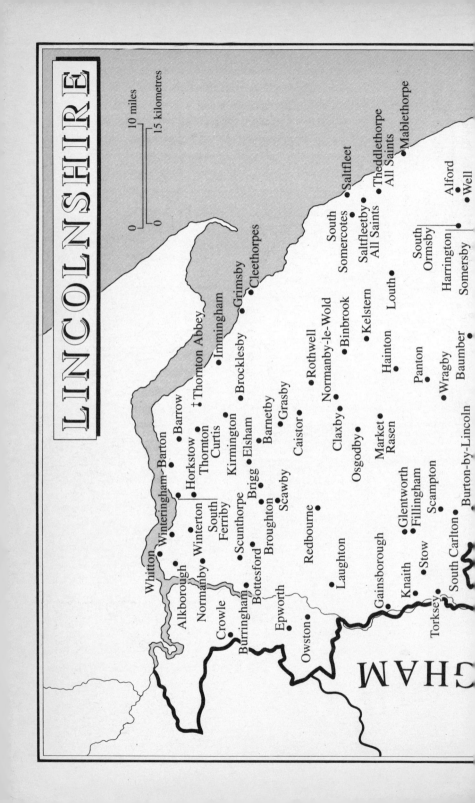

# Introduction

Lincolnshire is a county of surprises. 'You live in Lincoln-shire?' people will say (half incredulously). 'You live in Lincolnshire?' One always knows what is coming next: 'Very flat, isn't it?' 'Do you know Lincolnshire?' one may retort. 'Have you ever been there?' 'Oh no,' comes the reply, 'never.' One groans at the ignorance. Lincolnshire is an enormous, empty, unknown county, and herein lies its charm. It is a county of surprises.

Who knows Lincolnshire? Who knows the rolling country of the Stone Belt, to the south-west of the county around Grantham, stretching as far south as Stamford, with stone-built villages, stone-built manor houses, churches with broach spires? Who knows the Cliff, the line of hills which leads to Lincoln, where warm red brick joins Ancaster stone to form those colourful villages, dominated, every one, by handsome churches? Who knows the country north of Lincoln, where the long straight road, the Ermine Street, leads on for mile after endless mile along the Cliff to the Humber? Who knows the Wolds, those rolling chalk downs, with endless tiny valleys hung with beech woods, with small villages, with tiny, often very ancient, churches, which stretch from the Humber in the north, as far south as Spilsby and Horncastle? Who knows Lincolnshire, the long unfrequented lanes, the forgotten main roads where the whole countryside generates a feeling of unchanged peace-fulness?

Who knows the Fens, that great flat saucer which surrounds the Wash, which we share with Cambridgeshire and Norfolk, where are the grandest, greatest, most glorious churches of all, in endless profusion, raising their tall spires, and mighty towers to a limitless sky?

Lincolnshire is a county of surprises. Martin is a case in point, a somewhat bleak village, with a T. H. Wyatt church and a long wide curving street which suddenly drops down into the fen – that very narrow stretch of fen which stretches north from Tattershall. It is only four miles wide and stretches to the Witham – here quite a wide river. Cross this by Kirkstead Bridge, and we are in a different world.

There are woods, there are rhododendrons, the foothills of the Wolds are upon us, we are in Woodhall Spa. The unfortunate Mr Parkinson, steward to Sir Joseph Banks of Revesby, dug here hoping to find coal. All he found was spa water which has made Woodhall Spa; while poor Mr Parkinson is largely forgotten.

'Woodhall Spa', wrote John Betjeman, 'that most un-expected Bournemouth-like settlement in the middle of Lincolnshire'. Exactly. There are good shops, grand hotels – one, the Petwood, with a magnificent garden laid out by Harold Peto, another, the Golf, close to the celebrated golf course, one of the most famous in the country.

There is another Lincolnshire surprise, only a mile or so away, but difficult to find – for strangers. A country lane, leading to nowhere in particular, accompanies a plantation of oak trees: in front of this stands the Wellington Monument, an obelisk 36 feet high, surmounted by a bust of the Iron Duke. It was erected in 1844 by Colonel Richard Elmhirst of West Ashby Grove, one of Wellington's colonels at Waterloo. The inscription records that the wood (known as the Waterloo Wood) was planted 'From Acorns Sown Immediately After The Memorable Battle of Waterloo'.

The Elmhirsts of West Ashby and Stixwould were a branch of the Elmhirsts of Elmhirst in the West Riding of Yorkshire, the family which produced Mr Leonard

Elmhirst who, with his wife Dorothy, created Dartington Hall in Devon.

The final surprise in this part of Lincolnshire must be Mr Stockdale's exquisite opera house, the Music Pavilion of Thorpe Tilney, where Pavilion Opera was founded. But more of this in Chapter I.

Indeed the first eleven chapters – the 'Viewpoints' – all describe Lincolnshire surprises. The final surprise must be Lincolnshire itself.

# I

# The View from Thorpe Tilney

We are standing at the garden door of Thorpe Tilney Hall. Thorpe Tilney is one of those perfect mid-Georgian houses, that are to be found adorning our English countryside, built of warm red brick, with a Venetian window above the door, a lunette in the pediment above that, sash windows everywhere.

At Thorpe Tilney the show front faces west across the garden; if it were once the entrance front, good sense over the centuries has reversed the order, and the main door now is on the plainer east; plainer it may be, but attractive, too, with a pair of Venetian windows here, the broad sweep of grass bordered by old trees stretching to the road, and with a handsome and imposing stable block on the north side, pedimented and crowned with a cupola and clock. Through its central arch the drive now makes its way from the road, between immensely tall beech hedges, and up to the front door. Inside, a smaller hall with an elegant staircase leads into the grander hall, and so to the garden door itself, with steps leading down into the garden.

Here the visitor will stand spellbound: a fountain is playing in the centre of the lawn. There are mature trees to right and left, yew hedges at a distance on either side – and then the central vista. Here a wide avenue of lime trees leads the eye into the distance; young lime trees, perhaps fifteen, perhaps twenty years old, and, in the farther distance, still younger trees. It is like an eighteenth-century view by Kip; one of those incredible landscapes embracing (it might seem) a thousand acres or more, with young avenues

4

marching off in every direction, in perspective from the house. Did these landscapes ever exist, one is tempted to ask? Were these avenues, planted apparently to the end of the earth, really ever planted? Here is one such, and our pleasure is unbounded. It is as though we were back in the eighteenth century, witnessing their great tree planting schemes again.

But this is not all; half-concealed in the trees on the left is another building, apparently eighteenth-century, in brick, square, and crowned with a low octagon, local pantiles covering the octagon and the building itself, Diocletian windows in the four sides of the octagon complete this most interesting, unusual building. But what is it? It is, in fact, the Music Pavilion, or Opera House, designed by Francis Johnson, and built in 1975 and following years for Mr F. M. Stockdale. It is an exquisite little building, built of old brick from the walled garden of Leadenham House, and roofed with old brick pantiles from local cowsheds. Inside, all is white and glistening with gold, the gallery railings with elegant wrought iron banisters, the four lunette windows below the dome filled with glass by John Piper.

Thorpe Tilney is the home of Pavilion Opera, Mr Stockdale's own opera company; this incredibly beautiful little Music Pavilion is its base, and where it all started. In his fascinating book, *Figaro Here, Figaro There*, Freddie Stockdale describes a year in the life of his opera company. He became absorbed with opera when he was up at Cambridge, and conceived the idea of founding a small opera company. In 1971, he bought Thorpe Tilney, and in his vision saw an opera house built in the garden, as it is now, and grand avenues radiating from the house, as they do today. When he was at Eton, he sat at one time in chapel opposite a John Piper window; hence the idea of four Piper windows to adorn the dome of the opera house at Thorpe Tilney. They illustrate four scenes in the life of St Paul and they are among John Piper's most delightful works.

In the past ten years Mr Stockdale has taken Pavilion Opera to perform all across the world, not only at Thorpe Tilney, but in London and country houses throughout Britain, at Versailles and across Europe, in Australia and in India, in Canada and America, in fact in five continents. But they come back to Thorpe Tilney.

The opera house still is not all. Behind our shoulders as we gaze across the view from the garden door, to the south-east of the house, is the most tremendous walled garden; it comprises, of course, a whole series of gardens, all separated by little box hedges, for flowers or vegetables, fruit trees and bushes, and at the far end stands the most delectable little eighteenth-century garden house or orangery, with long sash windows, its Dutch pediment crowned with an urn. The outside world is shut out from here, by its all-embracing, magnificent, brick wall.

Penetrating outside it is possible to absorb the view to the south and the east, so different from the view to the west. Here the prospect is across the wild fen, the rich black-soiled fen, which stretches from within a few miles of Thorpe Tilney right across to the Wash, to Norfolk and Cambridgeshire. Great landmarks stand out: the tremendous Tudor brick tower of Tattershall Castle, the tower of its grand collegiate church next door, Coningsby church tower beyond, and, on a clear day, Boston Stump beyond that.

This view is in marked contrast to the view towards the west. Here the prospect, aided by Mr Stockdale's avenues, leads the eye to the civilised world of the Lincoln Heath and the Lincoln Cliff, an entirely different world of stone villages and country houses, on to Lincoln itself, with its colossal cathedral on its own hill fifteen miles away.

There is yet another view from Thorpe Tilney. On a clear day, looking north-east, we can take in another prospect: the Lincolnshire Wolds, those little known chalk hills which reach from the Humber, to the north, and come tumbling down to the marsh and the fen, south of Horncastle and Spilsby. Thorpe Tilney is more or less the centre of Lincolnshire; the ideal place to begin our survey of the county: it is typical of Lincolnshire – unassuming, unpretentious, but wonderful. Moreover, like so many things in the county, it is totally unexpected, a tremendous surprise. Whoever would have expected to find an opera house here, indeed the home of an internationally known opera company?

Mr Stockdale, of course, is the creator of Thorpe Tilney as we know it now. But who was the original creator of this magic little kingdom? To discover his identity we have to go over to Aswarby, on the far side of Sleaford. Here in the church, among monuments to other members of his family, is one 'To the memory of Francis Whichcote of Timberland Thorpe Esquire youngest son of Sir Francis Whichcote Baronet and Dame Frances his wife, who died October 19th 1784, aged 46 years'. If not its builder (because it could have been built by his father) Francis Whichcote must have been its first occupant. The Whichcotes owned Timberland and Timberland Thorpe (alias Thorpe Tilney) from the early eighteenth century: their shield adorns the village school in Timberland – ermine, two boars passant gules, – and Aswarby still belongs to the family.

Nor must it be forgotten that 'Aswarby Hall, in the heart of Lincolnshire' was the scene of M. R. James' most terrible ghost story – 'Lost Hearts'. Why did Monty James choose Aswarby? The answer is that he had been at Eton with Sir George Whichcote (the ninth Baronet). And why was the villain of the story Mr Abney? A glance at a map will show that a wood, on the edge of the estate, is marked 'Abney's Wood'.

The roads from Thorpe Tilney lead off to most diverting places; through Timberland and Martin, the road dips down into the fen, and so on to the Witham. Over the

Witham, and the countryside changes dramatically; there are pine trees and silver birches and thick woods, and we are in Woodhall Spa. Another road leads to Kirkstead Abbey, its gaunt grim fragment of the south transept still standing, with Kirkstead Chapel, the *capella ante portas* of the famous Cistercian Abbey, one of the two or three most beautiful churches in Lincolnshire; another to Tattershall. Here that most magnificent of Tudor castles, thanks to Lord Curzon, still stands, and nearby, the very fine Collegiate Church, also built by Ralph, Lord Cromwell. The road west from Thorpe Tilney leads to Scopwick, a pretty village with a stream running through the village street of stone cottages – Lincolnshire's reply to Bourton-on-the-Water. Were this the Cotswolds, people would come running; but this is Lincolnshire, dull, flat, boring Lincolnshire, so no-one comes, thank God.

# II
# The View from Monksthorpe

Spilsby, Halton Holgate, Great Steeping, Irby in the Marsh, Thorpe St Peter, Wainfleet: the road descends from the Wolds to the Marsh. At Great Steeping there is a lane leading north, to Candlesby and Gunby and Bratoft, but, half a mile on, another lane turns off to the right marked 'No through road' which leads to a farm, and, beyond the farm, to a curving drive, planted with lime trees. What is this? It is Monksthorpe Baptist Chapel, the oldest Baptist chapel in Lincolnshire, and one of the oldest in England. It is a small rectangular gabled building of mellow plum-coloured brick, with sash windows and pantiled roof, at present undergoing restoration, its south wall till recently propped up. It was built in 1701, and was in regular use by this old Baptist community till recently – indeed, as the flowers on the graves in the churchyard reveal, people are still buried here and this spot is regarded as a holy place.

It is, moreover, a very beautiful spot, with old trees all round the churchyard; a screen, a protecting wall as it were against the outside world. The lawns are all beautifully mown – an act of *pietas* on somebody's part – and, most moving of all, there is behind us as we survey the chapel the place of Baptism, a small rectangular pool in the garden with steps down for those to be baptised. This is one of the very few outside baptismal pools to survive in all England, and it is of immense interest.

The Baptist community here is quite ancient, having been founded by Thomas Grantham of Halton Holgate, the early and most formidable seventeenth-century Baptist leader,

9

who obtained an interview with Charles II in 1660; nonetheless he was imprisoned for preaching in 1662, and again in 1670. He also founded Baptist communities at King's Lynn and Norwich, but died in 1692, before the Monksthorpe chapel was begun, indeed before the building of non-conformist chapels became legal.

Driving away from this beautiful, holy, place we become aware not merely of farm buildings but of great hangars, which formed part of the wartime R.A.F. station here. It was to extend the runway here that the R.A.F. sought in 1943 to demolish Gunby Hall, which lay in the way. It was the home then of Field-Marshal Sir Archibald Montgomery-Massingberd, who had until quite recently been Chief of the Imperial General Staff. He raised the issue with the Secretary of State for Air, then with the Prime Minister – who were both sorry that nothing could be done – but the Field-Marshal was not a courageous soldier for nothing, and he took the matter to the King, who said of course something could and would be done about it. So the line of the runway was redrawn by a few inches; by the time it reached the radius of Gunby Hall, it was a hundred yards or more from the house; the National Trust assisted with negotiations, and as a thank-offering the Field-Marshal and his wife gave the place to the nation; thus was one of the most enchanting of all Lincolnshire houses saved, and one of its most beautiful gardens.

It is fascinating to reflect that Gunby was built by Sir William Massingberd in 1700, just a year before Monksthorpe Chapel. They are both built of the same mellow plum-coloured brick.

Monksthorpe, like Thorpe Tilney, is a beautiful place from which to drive through quiet lanes to interesting places nearby; from the main gate to Gunby it is but a stone's throw to the old railway station of Burgh-le-Marsh on the now defunct East Lincolnshire main line. In earlier, happier days we could have boarded a train here and travelled north, to Alford and Louth, or south to Boston and Spalding and distant King's Cross. The line was senselessly closed down in 1970. The charming railway station of Burgh, like a dignified late Georgian farmhouse, is now a tea shop, and a railway museum occupies the adjoining buildings.

We must be content with the road, which leads east to Burgh-le-Marsh itself, a captivating little place with winding street and diminutive market place, a six-sailed windmill in working order and a grand Perpendicular church with great tower crowned with lofty pinnacles. From here the dual carriageway across the marsh carries a great flood of traffic to Skegness, which has been described as a seaside suburb of Nottingham or Leicester. It was a quiet watering-place in the early nineteenth century, but the coming of the railway altered all that. At the south end is the one old hotel, The Vine, and the road leads to Gibraltar Point, which is the Nature Reserve of the Lincolnshire Naturalists' Trust. Here the Steeping River runs into Wainfleet Haven, and so into the Wash; in fact here the north side of Wainfleet Bay is the northern shore of the Wash.

Wainfleet is the oddest little place, but endearing, and indeed hallowed as the birthplace (c. 1395) of William of Waynflete, brought up at William of Wykeham's foundations of Winchester and New College, then transferred by Henry VI to Eton as Fellow of Eton (1440), and then second Provost (1443), and later Bishop of Winchester, Lord Chancellor of England, and founder of Magdalen College, Oxford. There is a little Market Square, and an extremely odd narrow street called Barkham Street, formed of tall terrace houses, as though it were in Paddington. But Magdalen College School was founded by William and is a distinguished little building of Tudor brick; and there is another building of importance: Bateman's Brewery, where Bateman's Good Honest Ales are brewed. The railway station is a lifeline to the outside world, the sole remaining branch of the old East Lincolnshire Railway, the line that leads to Skegness.

The blackest of soil, great fields of cabbages and Brussels sprouts in winter, surround Wainfleet; this landscape is perhaps an acquired taste. We can make our way back to the Wolds and visit Spilsby, an altogether delightful little town, with a long market place, and a parish church that has all the early tombs of the Willoughbys of Eresby – a series which is continued at Edenham, near Grimsthorpe (*q.v.*); only one splendid, solitary, gatepier remains of Eresby House, burned down in 1769, at the end of the long ancient avenue which leads from Spilsby.

There are grand churches to explore all around: Croft, close to Wainfleet, and Wainfleet St Mary, too, Halton Holgate near Spilsby, Friskney, Wrangle, Old Leake and Sibsey, where the marsh gives way to the fen.

# III
# The View from Osgodby

Few would suspect, on passing through the village of Kirkby-cum-Osgodby that here was the oldest Roman Catholic church in Lincolnshire. A number of nineteenth-century brick houses of the usual Lincolnshire type, a few twentieth-century bungalows of very familiar un-Lincolnshire type, the usual cottage gardens, and at the west end of the village, the parish church, in origin medieval; but where is the presence of Rome?

It is sometimes told how Mr Weld of Lulworth in Dorset persuaded George III, over a particularly good bottle of port, to allow him to build a Catholic chapel for his family and dependents. 'You may', declared the King, 'on condition that it doesn't look like a church.' Hence, across those great smooth lawns at Lulworth, amid their backing of beech trees, and high above the sea, there rose that handsome, square, stone building with its dome and sash windows.

Here, at Osgodby, there is an ordinary-looking house, its front facing south away from the street – but on its back wing, nearest the street, the observant visitor will notice a cross – and also notice that the tall upstairs windows contain stained glass. George III would almost have been satisfied.

The caretaker lives downstairs, but she will be pleased to show the church to sympathetic visitors: the steep staircase leads into a spacious upper room where a classical arcade divides the small sanctuary from the congregation. It is a holy place, steeped in the prayers of the faithful these past two hundred years. The Youngs of Kingerby and members of other old recusant families were the founders, though the Catholic mission at Market Rasen is older, and goes back to penal days. Fr. Edmund Thorold, S.J. the author's (collateral) ancestor served the mission there until his death in 1728.

Osgodby must be one of the least known places in one of the least known parts of the county. All around us here is that no man's land where Toft-next-Newton practically adjoins Newton-by-Toft, and in that no man's land is what must be the capital of no man's land, Snarford. Here there is a handful of cottages, a farmhouse, and a small church – from the outside, at any rate – of little consequence. There is nothing else, and it is in the middle of nowhere. Within the church there are pews, and there is an altar, but the whole building is dominated by huge Elizabethan tombs. Behind the altar is one great tomb, occupying the entire chancel – to Sir Thomas and Lady St Paul (1582) and in the north chapel, another enormous tomb to Sir George St Paul and his wife and daughter (1613). His wife was Frances Wray (of Glentworth), and she subsequently married Robert, Earl of Warwick – so there is a second monument to her with her second husband, with medallion portraits of them both as though they were looking out of a carriage window. This is an enchanting and unusual monument. There are other smaller memorials, but the St Pauls are gone, as though they had never been; there is now but the farmhouse on the site of their once great house.

There is another great collection of family monuments nearby, at Hainton, to the Heneages, and indeed a greater collection, starting earlier, and continuing to our own days, because, happily, the family survives, and is still here in residence; but more of Hainton in Chapter XVII.

Market Rasen is an agreeable, but inconsequential little town, with a small market place, a railway station on one of the few lines across the county which Dr Beeching has left us, and the race course; the thing to do is to take the road north (A46) to Caistor, and turn off after a few miles to Claxby and, beyond that, climb the hill to Normanby-le-Wold. This is a thrill, with a view of the whole county to west and north, and another tremendous view from the churchyard to the south; all the usual landmarks can be identified. A little to the north is Caistor, which must have once been a Roman station, now a pleasantly decayed little town with a sloping market place, and, beyond again, rising through the thick woods which crown the Wolds, stands Pelhams' Pillar, built in 1849 to commemorate the planting of twelve million trees by the first Lord Yarborough. Brocklesby, Lord Yarborough's great demesne, is beyond: a park of a thousand acres, the house, the kennels, the church and Wyatt's superb mausoleum, beyond this. But Brocklesby itself is also dealt with at greater length in Chapter XVII.

All the roads between here and Binbrook are a delight and lead in every direction to countryside of wonderful beauty and remoteness. The best road of all is the High Street, which leads right along the spine of the Wolds from Caistor to Horncastle, passing no village in all its twenty-four miles.

# IV
## The View from Well Vale

We are sitting in the portico of Well Church. It is a simple, sturdy, stately portico of Roman Doric columns bearing a wide pediment crowned with a cupola, and the seats placed on either side of the doorway command one of the best views in Lincolnshire. The church stands on a grassy knoll of the park, a grassy knoll of the Wolds, as they come tumbling down into the marsh. All around us are grand and ancient trees, beech and ash and oak; as we look down from the hillside we see first the eighteenth-century mansion in its garden setting, with the park continuing beyond, the whole demesne watered by streams and pools and large sheets of water – all fed by the wells from which the place takes its name. Also, beyond the park, we see the farms and cottages of marshland – and, beyond, the coastline, hazy perhaps on a summer day, and then the sea, shimmering in summer sunshine. Inside, the church is perfect, with its original furnishings of pews set college-chapel wise, its altar rails and handsome three-decker pulpit; on the front of the gallery hang a set of eighteenth-century hatchments bearing the arms of the Bateman, Chaplin and Dashwood families. It is all specially attractive with its green light from surrounding trees through clear glass windows. The house itself is perfect, too, and perfect for its setting, built of plum-coloured brick, of two storeys, with a wide central pediment, low parapet with dormers, and widely spaced sash windows on ground and first floors; the front door stands open in the centre.

The house was built *circa* 1725 by James Bateman,

brother of the first Lord Bateman who at Shobdon in
Herefordshire created another (but no more beautiful)
landscape park, and built a most exotic Gothick church; so
it is to these two brothers that we owe two rare eighteenth-
century churches. We can descend and approach the house,
the open front door bidding us enter. The house is spacious,
airy, with staircase ascending to a gallery; ahead, aligned on
the front door and set in its vaulted alcove, is the garden
door, with a view of lakes and gardens; on the right, a long
and lovely room with windows facing east and west and
south, to command the view all round, classical columns to
divide the room informally – it is, as it were, almost an
eighteenth-century long gallery – with drawing-room at the
west end, with a view of the church standing like a little
classical temple on its low hill; dining-room at the far end
with a view across the lawn and lake. Well Vale is the most
beautiful setting of any house in Lincolnshire.

The little town of Alford is but a short distance, with its
market place, thatched manor house, spacious medieval
church, five-sailed windmill in working order and an
imposing Italianate railway station – but no railway. It was
part of the East Lincolnshire line, so senselessly destroyed in
1970. The station is approached by a roadway marked
'Beechings Way'. Beeching has had his way all right, to the
great loss of us all.

Beyond the little town the marsh stretches out: to the
coast, to Mablethorpe, famed for its sands but itself little
more than a 'shack town'. There are wonderful churches on
the marsh: Theddlethorpe All Saints, Saltfleetby All Saints,
Skidbrook. And the spire of Louth beckons us.

Everyone should walk up Westgate in Louth to gaze at
the spire; but the whole town is a pleasure with its streets of
Georgian brick houses. And from here we can explore the
countryside behind us: the countryside between Alford and
Spilsby and Horncastle, the countryside of the Wolds,
perhaps the most beautiful part of Lincolnshire, with its tree

hung hills, its valleys and tiny villages. And in its own valley is Somersby, birthplace of Tennyson. There are interesting memorabilia of the great man in the church, but the place is gloriously uncommercialised and very private, in fact much as it must have been when the Revd George Tennyson came to be Rector here in 1806. There is more about the Tennyson family in chapter XVI.

# V

# The View from the Burton Shatoo

Driving along the road from Lincoln to Gainsborough (A156), it will hit us in the eye: an elegant little eighteenth-century Gazebo, standing against a background of splendid trees in the park at Gate Burton. It is a perfect little building of brick and stone, with the entrance in the low, rusticated ground floor, the main rooms in the piano nobile above; Ionic pilasters, urns above the cornice, a hipped roof behind the parapet, the lower side wings with their own hipped roofs, urns and parapets – it is a beautiful little composition. Its purpose from the road may not at first be apparent, but driving towards it across the park will explain all: it is built dramatically overlooking the Trent, at a point where the great river makes a sweeping bend, and looks upstream to Littleborough where the Romans had a ford to take the Till Bridge Lane from Ermine Street, across towards Doncaster.

Gate Burton Hall stands in the other half of the park across the road, and is itself an interesting building, half of 1765, a plain house of white brick built by the Huttons; the other half, backing it, much grander in red brick and stone, built by Detmar Blow for the Sandars in 1913. It is now flats. The Gazebo – known as the Burton Shatoo (= Chateau) – belongs to the Landmark Trust and is, of course, available for holiday letting. Whether a Landmark holiday is required or not, the Burton Shatoo makes an ideal place from which to explore another corner of the county. It is an historic corner, full of treasures.

To the south is Doddington, one of the most splendid of Elizabethan or Jacobean houses – and one of the most beautiful, with its gatehouse and walled gardens, all built of mellow red brick. There is more of this in Chapter XVI. Just off the main road is Kettlethorpe, with its late medieval gatehouse – which once served as the gatehouse to the vanished medieval house of the Swynfords: Katherine Swynford was third wife of John of Gaunt.

A mile or two to the north is Fenton, where there are old warehouses, a lock and a wharf along the Fossdyke Navigation, a relic of nineteenth-century industrialisation; soon after, the Fossdyke flows into the Trent, and we reach Torksey (pronounced 'Torsey').

Torksey is fascinating. It was once a small town on the Trent, with two churches and two religious houses (a priory of Augustinian Canons, and a small Benedictine nunnery); one small church survives, and on the east bank of the Trent, much grander than the church, the ruined façade of the so-called Torksey Castle. In fact it was the mansion of the Jermyn family, built here on the Trent in the late sixteenth century by Sir Robert Jermyn. The family gave their name to Jermyn Street (London SW1), and their principal seat was at Rushbrooke in Suffolk. Their beautiful house there, of much the same date as Torksey, was later charmingly Georgianised, but was wantonly destroyed in the early 1960s; Torksey had been nearly destroyed in the Civil War and never rebuilt. It stands like a wonderful piece of stage scenery in a field of cows, here by the river, half-concealed from public view by the village street.

North of the village, a signpost points to Brampton, another romantic spot, where 'Torksey Ware' was made in the very early nineteenth century, by William Billingsley, 'one of the most remarkable characters in English Art'.

Porcelain was first made in England in the mid-eighteenth century, the great manufactories being at Chelsea and at Bow, the 'poor man's Chelsea'. Billingsley was born in 1753, at Derby. His father was in porcelain, and had come from Chelsea to Derby. William spent his life dedicated to the manufacture and decoration of porcelain, and he became famous for his special gifts and techniques: he joined Mr Coke, Squire of Pinxton (Derbyshire), in the manufacture and decoration of Pinxton Ware, which is especially beautiful and rare. Later, Billingsley moved to Mansfield and then to Torksey; Torksey Ware being rarer still and jealously collected.

Brampton is a very attractive hamlet of eighteenth-century houses, and close to the river is the site of the Manufactory, an elegant late-Georgian block with bottle kiln behind, as it appears on some pieces of his porcelain. There is nothing left there now – just the site on the higher ground above the river, with a path leading down to the water's edge where a little canal led to the wharf. The site of the Manufactory has been excavated, and measurements taken of the foundations of the building – which include the bottle kiln – so the Torksey Ware must have been made here by Billingsley, as well as decorated by him. French ware and other ware were also brought here, to be decorated.

Alas, all ended in disaster. Billingsley never had any money of his own, and the principal partner, Mr Bankes, an attorney of Lincoln, who had already been behind Pinxton ware, went bankrupt. Torksey seemed the ideal site, on the Trent, with ready access everywhere by water, but after six years all was shut down, and Billingsley departed for Worcester and then South Wales. It is a lonely site today, with the great phalanx of cooling towers of the Cotham Power Station belching forth on the Nottinghamshire bank opposite, and the cows grazing silently around; but a glance at the map will be of interest: the farm at the corner of the lane to the village is named Pottery Farm.

The next village north (if one can call it a village) is Knaith, which lies a mile or two downstream. The little church here is a fascinating fragment of a Cistercian nunnery and is situated right upon the river bank. Across the lawn is the Hall, a long, low, old house, done up early in the nineteenth century in Regency Gothic. Thomas Sutton, founder of the Charterhouse, as well as the famous school, was born here in 1532. The road leads on to Gainsborough.

Gainsborough is St Oggs in *The Mill on the Floss*, the little inland port on the Trent, with its old warehouses on the river bank and its little narrow streets which lead suddenly to one of the finest medieval manor houses to survive in England. Its survival is amazing (see also Chapter XIV). There is also a very good Georgian parish church built by Francis Smith of Warwick (1736– 44).

From the centre of the great plain to the south-east of the town, rises the grand fortress-like Saxon and Norman church of Stow, its own obscure little village clustering round giving it a delightfully French look. Traditionally the Minster Church of the Saxon See of Sidnacester, it was burnt by the Danes in 870, and rebuilt by Eadnoth, Bishop of Dorchester (in whose Diocese Lincoln then lay) shortly before the Conquest. A mile or two to the east, far away in its fields, with a large farm for company, stands the tiny church of Cotes-by-Stow, with its splendid medieval rood screen. (For both Cotes and Stow see also Chapter XV on the churches of Lincolnshire.)

# VI
# The View from Croyland

Like the hulk of an enormous wrecked ship, the ruins of
Croyland Abbey (now generally spelt Crowland) loom
upon the horizon – the flat landscape of the deepest
Lincolnshire fens. This was the spot to which St Guthlac
came on St Bartholomew's Day, 699. Tired of soldiering,
Guthlac, a member of the Mercian royal house, had entered
the monastery of Repton, and after two years of study
determined to become a hermit. He vowed that he would
found his hermitage on whatever island in the swamps of
the Wash his boat became stranded. Croyland was that
place. In the tympanum of the Early English west door of
the ruined nave there is a quatrefoil reflecting events in the
life of the saint, one of which depicts the scene of his arrival
here in 699.

Croyland is a holy place in that remote fenland where
holy men came before the Conquest to withdraw from the
world; the former abbeys of Ramsey, Thorney, and
Peterborough are all in close proximity. Croyland seems an
odd, eerie, withdrawn little town even now. As we
approach from the west, from the civilisation of Market
Deeping and Stamford, and make our way along by the side
of the long, straight, canal-like River Welland for mile after
straight mile, we can see the solid tower of the abbey
crowned with its stumpy spire, silhouetted against the flat
skyline. The west front of the church is of great beauty,
albeit part wrecked, and still glorious with a host of original
canopied statues, a smaller version of Wells Cathedral. The
nave is a ruin, but the mammoth tower leads into an aisle,

still the parish church of Croyland, where a lamp burns before the high altar, and where prayers are still said. The spirit of St Guthlac seems never far away.

At the crossroads in the little town stands one of the greatest of curiosities: Croyland Bridge, the triangular bridge with its three arches meeting at the centre, that took travellers from the three streets that met here over the three streams of the River Welland. All are dry now. The bridge is fourteenth-century but is apparently the successor to an earlier Norman bridge of similar plan. It adds much to the atmosphere of the place.

And for atmosphere Croyland must be visited. Here can be savoured the unique flavour of fenland. Long, straight roads accompanied by long, straight dykes, the occasional misshapen, stumpy tree, the occasional linear settlement, the endless vast fields, the unending flat landscape, the distant horizon that never gets any nearer. Under this enormous sky – and it is a case of two thirds of every eyeful being sky – there stand those spires of some of the most amazing churches ever built. They are everywhere, and the road from Croyland leads out to them – to Gedney and Long Sutton, to Holbeach and Moulton, Quadring and Algarkirk, Swineshead and Donington, Sutterton, Frampton and Fleet. (See also Chapter XV.)

There is Surfleet, too, leaning six feet out of the perpendicular, looking precarious by the main road. There are great towers also, like Pinchbeck and Whaplode, Weston and Wigtoft, Bicker and Kirton and Gedney Hill. In the fens the churches sail past like ships at sea.

Spalding is a Dutch-like town where the River Welland sweeps through in a deep tidal channel. Each river bank is adorned with a terrace of dignified Georgian houses. The Dutch character has been accentuated in this century by the introduction of bulb growing and the whole neighbourhood is ablaze with flowers in spring. Spalding has its own remarkable medieval church with its own great medieval spire. Next door to it stands Ayscoughfee Hall, part medieval, part eighteenth-century Gothick, now the Museum, but once the house of Maurice Johnson, founder in 1710 of the Spalding Gentlemen's Society, to which at one time belonged a number of eminent early eighteenth-century figures. And the Society still flourishes.

Holbeach, nearby, was the birthplace of William Stukeley, founder of the Society of Antiquaries of London. The road leads on to Long Sutton, a charming little town, and to Sutton Bridge, where the swing bridge leads across the Nene, on into Norfolk.

From the bridge across the Nene it is possible to look downstream to the mouth of the river. Here stand the two lighthouses, built by John Rennie, architect of Waterloo Bridge (*circa* 1830), to celebrate the draining of the Great Fens. They had rarely been used, and the sea had receded still further, when in 1933 Sir Peter Scott, the artist and ornithologist, acquired a lease of the East Lighthouse and it became his home for six years, until the outbreak of the war in 1939.

Peter Scott, son of Captain Robert Falcon Scott ('Scott of the Antarctic') had since childhood been passionate about wildlife. At school, at Oundle, he had been encouraged by his headmaster, Kenneth Fisher, in these pursuits and when he went up to Trinity College, Cambridge, he soon converted his bedroom in Great Court into an aviary. At Cambridge, his passion for the Fens developed, and he soon discovered the thrills of the Wash – and of the Lighthouses in particular. When he came down from Trinity he was able to acquire a lease of the East Lighthouse from the Nene River Catchment Board, for £5 a year; so he settled down to life, completely absorbed in the world of the Fens. The birds were his daily companions. Here, too, he painted – not only birds, but all wildlife, and portraits, and from here he toured the world in search of rare and endangered species. Encouraged by his godfather, J. M. Barrie, he also wrote.

Other companions at the lighthouse were the Customs officers who came twice a day half an hour before high tide, and left half an hour afterwards, and hailed every passing ship entering or leaving the harbour at Sutton Bridge. Another companion was 'Samphire Charlie' who occupied the basement, did odd jobs for him and collected cockles and mussels, as well as that delicacy of the Lincolnshire coast: samphire.

After the war, the receding sea had left his lighthouse high and dry, and he was invited to take over and develop a new World Wildlife Trust site on the Severn; so Slimbridge took over from Sutton Bridge. But it all began here, and a plaque on the old lighthouse records

SIR PETER SCOTT
Painter and Naturalist
lived here
1933 – 1939

Nearby, the 'Peter Scott Walk', which leads along the ten miles of this wild and remote coastline to the Ferry at West Lynn, was opened by him on 12 April 1989.

North of Holbeach, and bridging the Wash, is a rather different and very residential community of parishes called Holbeach St Matthew, Holbeach St Mark, Holbeach St Luke, Holbeach St John and Gedney Dawsmere – all with little Victorian churches (three by Ewan Christian), all with pretty quite un-fenlike villages, with hedges and gardens and good farmhouses and cottages. These were the 'new' villages of Holbeach Marsh. Here it is possible to find a lonely road which leads to the seabanks, whence we can climb up and inspect the Wash, and look across to Boston on one side, and Hunstanton, in Norfolk, on the other. But it is the same story everywhere – look at the map – the names tell everything: Gedney Drove End, Moulton Seas

End, Holbeach Bank, Gedney Dyke, Bedford Level; this is a part of England which is unique. The cloudscapes are wide and splendid; and there is a great expanse of stars at night.

# VII
# The View from Sempringham

'The Site of Sempringham Priory, lost in the fields of Kesteven,' wrote Professor David Knowles O.S.B. 'makes in its own way as striking an appeal to the imagination as that of Fountains or Glastonbury.'

Sempringham was the birthplace of the only English monastic order, the Gilbertines, named after St Gilbert who was himself born at Sempringham, in 1083, the son of a wealthy Norman knight who was Lord of the manor here. The Gilbertines, founded *circa* 1131, were a double order of men and women; the men following the Rule of St Augustine, the women that of St Benedict. They occupied adjacent houses and had separate cloisters, but they worshipped in the same church, albeit divided by a high wall, so that they could not see each other, but only hear each other's voices praising God. There were twenty-six houses in all, some for canons only, some for nuns, but mostly double houses where monks and nuns lived their own separate lives, but under one roof, offering their work and worship to God. Only their church at Old Malton survives in use, but there are important remains at Chicksands in Bedfordshire and at Mattersey in Nottinghamshire. But here at Sempringham not one stone of the old priory stands upon another – all is gone. The English genius for self-destruction!

But Sempringham is a moving, romantic spot. In summer, in this most gentle, undulating countryside, great cornfields embrace the fragments of the Norman village church, built by the saint's father, crowned by a Perpendicular pinnacled central tower, and bereft of chancel and transept. It is the church where the Gilbertine Order was founded and first established. A path from the road runs up to the church: there is a grand Norman south doorway, with a thirteenth-century oak door adorned with handsome contemporary ironwork. Inside, the nave is Norman and grand, the sanctuary a brave Victorian attempt by Edward Browning (1868).

The church stands quite alone; the village once stood to the north, but all has now vanished. The great Priory stood below to the south, but this has vanished too. On a dry summer day it is possible to look down the low hill and see the earthworks in the bumpy field; but these are not the marks of the Priory, but of the great mansion built here by Edward, Lord Clinton after the Dissolution. However, we know from excavations and from aerial photography that this was built on the site of the Priory. We know, too, that the monastic church was of the size of a cathedral of the proportions of (say) Chichester – as befitted the mother church of its Order. We can but imagine the impression made by this great establishment, here, at the very point where the low undulations of the stone belt gave way to the fens.

Taking the road (B1177) north from here, we can observe this countryside and pass a whole string of important churches: Billingborough, Horbling, Swaton, Helpringham, Great Hale, Heckington. Turning west, we pass another winner, Asgarby, and so back to Sleaford, a compact and orderly little market town, the capital of Kesteven, with yet another great church to preside over its market place. If we continue west we shall reach Ermine Street and Ancaster, as its name suggests once an important Roman station, famous for its stone. It is the stone from Ancaster which built these grand churches, built these pretty villages, farms and manor houses. The whole area between Ermine Street and the Kesteven boundary is the

Stone Belt; the road then leads south, converging on Stamford and Market Deeping.

One of the best roads is that south from Sleaford (A15), which takes us past such delightful places as Silk Willoughby and Aswarby. There is a wonderful wide view, just past the roundabout, where to the east we see the splendid pinnacled tower of Folkingham, and the very tall, broach spire of Walcot to the west. And the view continues even beyond Folkingham, over to Rippingale tower far away, with the spreading fens stretching on interminably beyond.

Nobody should hurry through Folkingham; it is all a delight, with its market place sloping down from the grand brick façade of The Greyhound at the top to the seventeenth-century manor house at the bottom, with the grim House of Correction round the corner. The road goes on to Aslackby (pronounced Azelby) and Bourne. Bourne is a charming little town, with the tower of the Augustinian abbey dominating all around. The road leads on to the attractive town of Market Deeping with its wide street of town houses.

Another road which should not be missed is the 'back road' to Stamford, which leaves Ermine Street close to Coldharbour, and (parallel with the A1) takes us through the pleasures of Boothby Pagnall and Bitchfield, Corby Glen and Edenham – with a breath-taking view of Grimsthorpe on the way. But the byways and back lanes will lead the discerning traveller to a host of unknown delightful places all across the Stone Belt – too many to mention, too precious to publicise – and all roads lead to Stamford, most beautiful of all English towns.

# VIII
# The View from Harlaxton Manor

Like everything else at Harlaxton, the front door is gargantuan: the handle, the key, the lock, the hinges, the door itself and everything about it; all seems designed to inspire awe in every arriving guest. The door opens, and we are admitted into a low atrium, solemn and portentous, with a grand triple Baroque archway on the left, leading up stone steps beneath immense scrolls and keystones, towards a bronze, balustraded staircase beyond. Light streams down these stairs, light from above, into this low mysterious hallway. It is a subtle, cleverly designed theatrical entry to the great house. On either side of the central arch a clutch of stone trophies, shields, swords and trumpets, is hung nonchalantly from each rusticated pillar, like a clutch of walking sticks in any normal mortal's house; a great marble urn on either side – and a third one ahead – are the only furnishings. We ascend the stairs to the lantern-like vestibule, glad to shake off the Stygian twilight below, as we enter the glories that await us above. Here is the State Dining-Room, ready for a banquet of the gods, with a thrilling view from the windows of the long straight drive, making its way through those colossal, immense gatepiers, through the gatehouse, past the Vanbrughian, walled kitchen garden, on and over the bridge which crosses the lake, and on to the archway and to the main road. Far ahead, and aligned on this view, is Bottesford spire; on the left, peeping over the trees on a neighbouring hill, the towers and pinnacles of Belvoir Castle.

The Dining-Room leads into the Great Hall, an immense

room, set apart for a gathering of the giants, and so to the Grand Staircase made of cedar wood. Here our eyes look up to what seems like a vision of heaven – where clouds and cherubs, billowing draperies, festoons, cords and tassels, adorn the sides of an ever ascending tower: caryatids hold aloft each passing balcony or gallery, shells and garlands hang from every cornice or entablature. At the very top is the blue sky, where Father Time appears twice, each time with his scythe: real scythes, each draped with a flag, one bearing a plan of Harlaxton Manor, the other with a cameo portrait of Mr Gregory himself. It is a scene to transport us to Bavaria, to the Baroque world of Zimmermann and the Assam brothers; but the portrait of Mr Gregory introduces us to the author of all this pomp and show, the shy, solitary figure of Mr Gregory, a wealthy, scholarly bachelor, who was not, as might be supposed, a self-made industrialist or nouveau riche, but an old established county squire, descended from a long line of old English de Ligne and Gregory ancestors, established at Harlaxton since the seventeenth century. What made him build the largest house in Lincolnshire is not known. Family pride; an extraordinary ambition to rival the great landowners who were his neighbours – for Grantham is surrounded by great family seats – Belvoir, Denton, Stoke Rochford, Easton, Belton, Syston; a natural flair for architecture and a collection of pictures that he had made on his travels? These may have been contributory causes. And yet? This little known man eludes us.

Harlaxton descended sideways for a century, then was put up for sale in 1937. This kind of house, this kind of architecture, was taboo just then; nobody wanted it except to pull it down. In desperation, the agents advertised it in *The Times*: 'To save from demolition, a purchaser required for Harlaxton Manor near Grantham. The labour of an age in piled stones, it ranks definitely as one of the stately homes of England. Ample suites of reception rooms, eighty bedrooms . . .' Mrs van der Elst came forward, bought it, and saved it. She should be canonised.

The next place to Harlaxton is Denton, the last village in Lincolnshire adjoining the Leicestershire border. With its handsome church and many pretty estate cottages it is altogether attractive. Sir Arthur Blomfield's Tudor gatehouse (1898) leads up a long avenue of ancient horse chestnuts to Denton Manor, seat of the Welbys. To a small early seventeenth-century nucleus, Mr Marshal Sisson and Mr Peter Foster have lately (1960) added a delightful new house, in keeping with the original; the park and setting are specially beautiful. There is more about Denton in Chapter XVI.

Grantham itself was a fine old market town which, as everybody knows, has been wrecked in recent years. Good Georgian streets, lined with houses of mellow brick, have been torn down. This policy of destruction – whosesoever it was – has been extraordinarily successful.

Round the parish church, things are better, with the delightful eighteenth-century vicarage and the King's School, founded by Bishop Fox of Winchester, founder of Corpus Christi College, Oxford, which has its original sixteenth-century quadrangle like a small Oxford college. And Grantham House, in origin the medieval house of the Hall family, transformed into a charming early eighteenth-century building, with panelled rooms and enchanting garden, now belongs to the National Trust. St Wulfram's, of course, is one of the great parish churches of England. Its wonderful spire, the earliest of all great English spires, is, according to Sir George Gilbert Scott, 'second only to Salisbury in beauty'.

This is a part of the county well endowed with good villages, manor houses and churches. Among the churches, Great Ponton comes to mind, as does South Stoke; among the manor houses, Woolsthorpe, where Newton was born. And the Great North Road leads south to Stamford.

North from Grantham, the main road to Lincoln (A157) follows the Cliff, and is strung with pretty villages and handsome houses. Belton comes first, the house serene and splendid, most beautiful of all late seventeenth-century English houses; the church filled with family monuments. Syston comes next, then Barkston, then a village every pretty mile, Caythorpe, with a compelling spire, and Fulbeck pre-eminent, both for its sloping street and its early eighteenth-century Hall, home of the Fanes, with its superb early eighteenth-century wrought iron gates and lime avenue; the church has a handsome many-pinnacled tower. Then comes Leadenham – with its great crocketed spire – with Leadenham House next door, a decided late eighteenth-century stone-built mansion, the home of the Reeve family. The road leads on, to Wellingore and Navenby, the former with its Norman revival Roman Catholic chapel attached to the Hall, the latter with its broad village street. And on to Coleby and Harmston – two worthwhile churches and an interesting Hall apiece – with a superlative Temple by Sir William Chambers in the garden at Coleby. And so to Lincoln.

But turning off at Barkston, we come to Marston and the Witham Valley. At Marston, a broach spire and the ancient house of the Thorolds next door; Hougham, with a splendid church; Westborough with another; up the hill to Hough-on-the-Hill to see its tower, one of only four Saxon towers with extruding staircases in all England; and the road leads north to Stragglethorpe and Brant Broughton. Stragglethorpe church must not be missed, a little early church, with an undisturbed eighteenth-century interior. Brant Broughton is one of the very best of all Lincolnshire churches, not only for its grand spire and fourteenth-century nave, but also for its nineteenth-century chancel by Bodley and all its furnishings and glass by him and Canon Sutton.

From Brant Broughton the lonely road leads on to

Lincoln; we should divert and stop to look at Norton Disney, the church filled with ancient Disney monuments, ancestors or at least collateral ancestors of the creator of Mickey Mouse, and then resume the road. Ahead is the great cathedral on its hill, and as we pass by every field along this empty, quiet road we see the great church ever more clearly. So we approach, in excitement and reverence. 'You can see ...... Cathedral in a day,' remarked Alec Clifton-Taylor once in an unguarded moment. (And the cathedral he mentioned was one of the very greatest of English cathedrals.) 'But you will need a week to see Lincoln.'

# IX

# The View from Thornton Abbey

Pottering in the uneventful lanes of northernmost Lincoln-shire, not far from the Humber, the great gatehouse suddenly comes in sight – overbearing, of towering height, inexplicable, it rears up at the end of a quiet lane, magnificent still, even five centuries after it was built. An explanation seems called for: is it military? The entrance to a vanished castle? Despite the arrow slits, the figures of saints – the Virgin, St Augustine of Hippo, and (perhaps) St John the Baptist – belie that and proclaim its character religious.

Thornton Abbey was founded for Augustinian Canons in 1139 – a priory first, but raised to abbey status nine years later, and becoming mitred in 1518. Its first monks came from Kirkham (in the East Riding). After the Dissolution, Henry VIII refounded it as a secular college, with dean, canons and schoolmasters, but it was suppressed once more by Edward VI. Sir Vincent Skinner purchased the place in 1610, and built a grand residence for himself between the gatehouse and the church, but for some unaccountable reason it all collapsed. 'It fell quite down to the bare ground without any visible cause', as a contemporary account put it. So much for tampering with a holy place. Successive owners followed and helped themselves to stone from church, college and mansion, so that now there is very little to see apart from the gatehouse, which must vie with St Osyth's in Essex and Battle in Sussex for the title of the grandest monastic gatehouse to survive.

The gatehouse is of stone and mellow brick, and was

begun *circa* 1380. It is approached by a barbican over one hundred feet long, across the moat, probably built in the sixteenth century after the founding of the college. Too little is known of this short-lived college, which must have resembled Henry's other foundation of Christ Church. The gatehouse is some indication of the importance of the abbey, which at the Dissolution still contained twenty-three canons. In 1541 Henry stayed three days, with his retinue, after the establishment of the college; one longs to know what was done to entertain the King.

Little is left of the church except for the fragment of the chapter house – a very beautiful fragment of the north and north-west walls of the octagon – but enough to show us that it must have resembled the chapter houses of York and Southwell, which both date from the end of the thirteenth century. There are a few remains of the buildings which stood around the cloisters, which have also vanished. The farmhouse to the south nearby is built above a vaulted undercroft, perhaps of the infirmary.

There is always something pathetic and sad about these holy places, where mortal man has striven to approach the Immortal; something very moving, too, even in their ruined state. We can sit or wander and absorb a little of the peace and beauty of the place.

Thornton makes an ideal place from which to explore north-east Lincolnshire. On the horizon, the hoists and cranes of Immingham, the tall chimneys of the chemical works and refineries that decorate the Humber bank, look menacing – perhaps an unexpected industrial invasion of what is otherwise an almost entirely rural county.

Immingham was the brainchild of the old Great Central Railway which decided in 1906 to defy Hull, across the water, and build here a dry dock which should be the wonder of the world. This was duly built and opened just before the outbreak of the First World War. New railway lines were built across these flat lands, and the Immingham tram, now sadly extinct, crept out along the coast from Grimsby. But the glory of Immingham was not yet to be. After 1918, the amalgamation of the railways meant the absorption of the Great Central Railway by the new London and North Eastern Railway which favoured Hull and Harwich. But now, in recent years, Immingham has come into its own, with the latest dock opened in 1960, and the port filled with ships from all over the world. But there is nothing to see, apart from the docks; there are merely the long roads of houses for employees, which so often tail off into nothing. Somewhat surprisingly, there is a fair-sized medieval church, and a few relics here of the old village. Close behind graze the calm cattle of Lincolnshire.

Grimsby is quite different: an ancient port and borough, which over the centuries has had its ups and downs of fortune. Once again it was the Great Central Railway which changed all this: new fish docks were built, and the fishing industry (which had languished in the seventeenth and early eighteenth centuries) revived. New industries arrived, and the population of fish and men leapt astronomically.

But the population grew so fast that there was little time to think or plan, and new, long streets were built, with very few distinguished buildings to grace them. There is the ancient and indeed magnificent medieval cruciform parish church, dating from the thirteenth century, and St Augustine's (in Legsby Avenue) is certainly worth a visit. It is of 1911 by Sir Charles Nicholson, and outwardly is not remarkable; but step inside. The nave is wide, the aisles wide also; the arcades and windows all with Nicolson's free Gothic details; it is a building of real atmosphere. Charmingly furnished, with pretty pews painted green and rood screen, it glows with flickering lamps and votive candles – the kind of church which compels one to one's knees.

But the most exciting building in Grimsby is undoubtedly the Dock Tower (1852), a hydraulic tower which rises in most spectacular fashion to a height of three hundred and nine feet. It is inspired by the tower of Siena Town Hall, but (one is tempted to say) it is bigger and better. The architect was J. W. Wild, of London. There is little else memorable in the town, but the tree-lined roads of large Victorian houses, built for the leading citizens of the nineteenth century, are an unexpected pleasure.

Cleethorpes is contiguous. The taste for sea-bathing first developed at the end of the eighteenth century, and the first hotels opened in the early nineteenth. Once again, it was the coming of the railway (in 1863) which was responsible for the great growth of the new seaside resort; the promenade was built, terraces of boarding houses constructed, new hotels established; pier, municipal gardens, children's paddling pools and all else followed. There is a large parish church, by the ubiquitous James Fowler (1867). The ancient parish church of Cleethorpes stands in what was the old village, a building of great importance, with Saxon tower and Norman nave; transepts and chancel are a little later, and their consecration by St Hugh in 1192 gives undoubted importance to the building.

But behind all this industry, and the swollen townships of Grimsby and Cleethorpes and their satellite villages, the Wolds survive unspoilt. One is suddenly aware of the great demesne and estate of Brocklesby, where the Pelhams, Earls of Yarborough, have been seated since Elizabethan times; indeed it was to free himself from the proximity of the Queen that the first Sir William Pelham, a younger son of the great Sussex family (now Earls of Chichester), came to these remote parts. Despite the proximity of Grimsby, they are still remote; the park itself is one thousand acres in extent, and a world apart. The great house, originally the rebuilding of a late Elizabethan or Jacobean house, was built *circa* 1730, but over the years has been much enlarged. It was the victim of a fire in 1898, and was rebuilt by Sir Reginald Blomfield and, more recently, reduced in size by

Claud Phillimore. The park was landscaped by Capability Brown, and the garden, with its lake, long walks and woodlands is adorned with temples and monuments, a grotto and a hermitage, and all that could be deemed essential to an eighteenth-century nobleman's pleasure ground. The extensive stables are close to the house, and the kennels of the celebrated Brocklesby hounds close to the church. Here are the earliest (and latest) family monuments; there is also a notable eighteenth-century organ in a beautiful case by James Wyatt.

But undoubtedly the finest building at Brocklesby is the Mausoleum. It stands at the end of a long ride in the park, among great cedar trees, and was built by James Wyatt in 1791 to the memory of the much loved wife of the first Lord Yarborough. And overlooking Caistor, rising from the great woodlands near Cabourne, stands Pelham's Pillar, already mentioned, built in 1849 to commemorate the planting of twelve million trees by Lord Yarborough.

At Goxhill, south of Barrow-on-Humber, is a fascinating house often called the Priory – which it never was. It is Goxhill Hall, and the tall medieval hall is indeed just that, with a captivating house of *circa* 1700 attached to it. It is a wonderful combination – the house filled with excellent late seventeenth- or very early eighteenth-century features – handsome staircase, and panelled rooms, together with the fourteenth-century hall and romantic moated garden. What more could be desired? Moreover, it belonged to the Hildyard family for centuries – and has now returned to them. So it can add continuity to all its other attractions.

# X

# The View from Alkborough

This is northernmost Lincolnshire. Stand in the churchyard
– alas, denuded of its tombs and headstones – and survey
the view, across the Humber to the Yorkshire hills beyond.
Here is the point where Ouse and Trent meet and become
the Humber. Or walk to Julian's Bower, a short distance to
the south-west – it is signposted – and inspect the maze cut
in the turf, and Countess Close nearby, a medieval earth-
work, and gaze from its bleak hillside across this remarkable landscape of rivers and flat lands to the west, all part of
the West Riding of Yorkshire. And look at the map –
Thorne Waste, Thorne Moors, Hatfield Chase, Hatfield
Moor. Goole Field, Goole Moor – or, nearer the rivers,
Addlingfleet, Swinefleet, Ousefleet, Yokesfleet. ('Fleet'
means a creek or inlet.) It is water that dominates the
landscape here. An aura of mystery and antiquity pervades
the place. The tower of the church is pre-Conquest, with an
Early English top; in the porch, let into the stone floor, is a
representation of the maze in iron.

We can make our way and follow the Trent, past Walcot
Old Hall, close to the road, a mid-seventeenth-century brick
house of great charm in what Sir John Summerson called
'artisan-mannerist style', three storeys high, with mullioned
windows, then make for Burton-on-Stather. 'Stather'
means 'landing place', and the stather here is below the
village, below the cliff, the landing place for the ferry across
the Trent. The churchyard here can detain us, as it did at
Alkborough, with its views across the Trent; across the
Ouse, to the great tower of Howden, as well as Selby or

York on a clear day. The church is Perpendicular with the monuments of the Sheffields of Normanby nearby. The family migrated from the Isle of Axholme in the sixteenth century to the more elevated countryside of Normanby, and a fascinating tablet in the chancel here describes how 'the venerable remains of the five Sheffields mentioned in the itinerary of Leland were rescued from the danger of oblivion ... by the not degenerate heir of that ancient family, John Earl of Mulgrave'. This was the third Earl, and – in course of time – first Duke of Buckingham and Normanby, friend of Dryden and Pope, and himself a man of letters.

The Dukedom expired in the next generation, but the family still survive as baronets and still run Normanby, though the main part of the great classical house (by Sir Robert Smirke in 1825) is now leased to Scunthorpe, as the town's Art Gallery and Museum – and a very fine gallery it makes. The family, though retaining one wing of the house, now make their principal home near York, escaping the smoke and fumes of Scunthorpe, the town which they helped to create.

Scunthorpe must seem a strange intrusion into agricultural, rural Lincolnshire. The discovery of iron ore here in 1858 – or rather, its rediscovery, for its existence was known to the Romans – resulted in this terrible conglomeration. What were five obscure villages suddenly developed into an enormous town of seventy thousand people. The long uninteresting streets of bright red brick, with all the usual shops and supermarkets, are dreary: the grand parish church by J. S. Crowther, built in 1889, was erected in the wrong place, and is at present unused and boarded up. So there is really very little to see. Round the medieval church of Frodingham (now the Parish Church of the town), some attempt at imaginative town planning has in recent years been made. There is a large central park, and here has been built the 'Civic Centre' and the Civic Theatre.

Joan Plowright is, after all, a native of Scunthorpe. But from a distance Scunthorpe can look magnificent, even extraordinary, with its chimneys and cooling towers and enormous, forbidding steel works, the more so at night when Vulcan's furnaces light up the heavens for miles around.

To the west of Scunthorpe, Keadby Bridge takes us across the wide, slow Trent, to the Isle of Axholme, the oddest, most remote, corner of Lincolnshire, bulging into Nottinghamshire, a land of rich summer grass, and deep winter mud, a black-earthed marsh, drained in the seventeenth century. Keadby Bridge was opened in 1916, and is a part road, part rail, swing bridge.

From here we can make a circuit of the Isle, taking the B road which keeps to the west bank of the river, to Althorpe, with its grand Perpendicular church, and then to Owston. Owston is perhaps the most attractive place in Axholme, with its imposing church, part Perpendicular, part early nineteenth century, and its street leading down to the river, full of atmosphere, like a Dutch painting. It was from here that the Earl of Mulgrave removed those remains of his ancestors, those early Sheffields, to Burton-on-Stather, in the eighteenth century. It is not far to Haxey, with its long street and imposing church, where the extraordinary Hood Game[1] is played on the Feast of the Epiphany each year.

But, again for atmosphere, take the road west from here to Wroot, which is the most westerly outpost of Lincolnshire, and as gaunt as its name. Here, John Wesley was curate to his father, the Rector of Epworth, though the bleak little red brick church is a Victorian replacement of the building in which he would have ministered. Thirty years ago there was a bungalow here named optimistically

---

[1] A game in which twelve 'boggins' or plough-boys and a 'fool' try to keep a hood or sackcloth in a particular field, while the rest of the players try to seize it, and take it to one of the local pubs, which offer rewards for it.

'Bella Vista', surveying the flat, featureless landscape of Hatfield Chase and Thorne Waste. It seems (1995) to have vanished, or been renamed.

Epworth, next door, is Wesley's birthplace: the handsome early eighteenth-century rectory now belongs to the Methodist Church and is open to the public. When Wesley revisited the place in 1742, debarred from the church, he preached to a great throng from his father's tomb on the south side of the chancel. Epworth is heavy with the air of non-conformity, but it is a not unattractive little town.

The road leads north to Belton – a scattered village, with a good medieval church – and so to Crowle, a big village, or small town, with a grand market square and a medieval church with an important (seventh-century) runic stone, carved with the figures of St Oswald, King of Northumbria, and his successor, King Oswin. There is also a beautiful little Roman Catholic church of St Norbert by M. E. Hadfield (1891).

This central spine of Axholme with its medieval settlements is undulating and must have formed a long island amid the waterlogged waste around. As we go north from Crowle we can almost reach the mouth of the Trent and the very flat lands that surround it, and make our way back, hugging the west bank of the river to Keadby Bridge once more.

Returning to the 'mainland' we can, briefly, take the east side of the river, to inspect a church by S. S. Teulon, now in the care of the Redundant Churches Fund. A building of rare ugliness, but special Teulonian character, with its extraordinary short west tower, and pyramidal spire, nave and chancel and apsidal sanctuary, all in drab red brick, marked out in black, it sits by the side of the river here, squat and assertive, solidly important, refreshingly original. It is worth a visit.

Another important church nearby is Bottesford, one of the most distinguished pure Early English churches anywhere; the nave is lofty and clerestoried, the chancel equally so. Everywhere there are long, narrow lancet windows, especially and strikingly so in the chancel. In the nave there is clever interplay of alternate circular windows. The church deserves to be better known. So does Laughton, further to the south, a 'Meynell church' (like Hoar Cross in Staffordshire), in this case a medieval building, glorious and decorated, added to by Bodley for Mrs Meynell-Lugram in 1896. This is remote, secluded countryside, with great woods in the care of the Forestry Commission.

From here we can make our way west, and climb back on to the Cliff. Redbourne is fun, with its little toy-fort Gothick gateway (by Carr of York) to the Hall, which was the seat of the Dukes of St Albans (descendants of Charles II and Nell Gwynne) inherited from the Carter family, to whom there are elegant eighteenth-century monuments in the church, a church resplendent with eighteenth-century plaster vaulting and a frightening stained glass window of the Day of Judgement by John Martin. This church is also in the care of the Redundant Churches Fund, and also should not be missed. And there is another important church, to the west of Brigg, at Broughton, with its Saxon tower and semi-circular extruding staircase turret.

Brigg is a little market town, now pedestrianised, so that no motorist can enter to enjoy its attractive buildings. The Grammar School was founded by Sir John Nelthorpe in 1674 the family still live nearby. The fame of the town is assured by the old folk song 'Brigg Fair', the music by Percy Grainger, and sung by Gervase Elwes.

So we can make our way back to the Humber. At Wrawby, just outside Brigg, is the very rare eighteenth-century Post Mill – the only one in the county, and splendidly restored in memory of Lady Winefrede Elwes, in 1965. Elsham, home of the Elwes family, is nearby (more of this on p. 108). We should take the road from here to South Ferriby (B1204); on the way, we shall pass through

Horkstow, which in any case has an interesting church, and a distinguished, miniature-grand eighteenth-century Hall. But, above all, this was the place where the painter of animals, George Stubbs, lived for several years in the 1750s, dissecting his horses and making accurate drawings of their anatomies. Here, too, is an unexpected suspension bridge designed by Sir John Rennie (1844), across the new River Ancholme; then the road descends suddenly, with views of the Humber below. The road west leads to Winterton and Wintringham, two large attractive villages with fine churches, and to Barton-on-Humber, an engaging little town with two ancient churches, one the celebrated Saxon church with its tiny nave and noble tower. We can survey the views of Hull opposite, and that incredible elegant white elephant, the Humber Bridge. This was begun in 1972 and was originally estimated to cost 28 million pounds. The total cost to date (1996) is £435 million. Was it worth it? For a heavy toll it carries a trifling volume of traffic in each direction every day.

There is a great picture by Stubbs, painted in 1776 and often reproduced in books, of Sir John Nelthorpe (the eighth Baronet) out shooting with two pointers on Barton Fields: a wonderful picture depicting this spacious exhilarating countryside. The little town of Barton-on-Humber lies below it with its two church towers, the grand sweep of the great estuary of Humber close behind.

# XI
# The View from West Keal

When Shell, a few years ago, produced their film of the Fens (in succession to a film of the Peak District) for their film library, it opened at West Keal. The cameras followed the line of the Wolds south-west of Spilsby, then left the main road and climbed the hill to West Keal church, standing so prominently on top, with its grand Perpendicular tower. (This actually fell in 1881, but was meticulously rebuilt, gargoyles and all.) Here the cameras entered the south porch, then turned round to embrace the incredible view: the panorama of the fens, from near Wainfleet to Sutton Bridge, and beyond (with the eye of faith) to the Norfolk coast, then round almost to Tattershall. It is indeed an incredible view: it made a wonderful introduction to the Fens, laid out like a great carpet before our eyes. In the centre of the horizon, unmistakable, is Boston Stump.

The main road to Boston (A16), via Stickney and Sibsey, leads off our road (A155); to the east, near the coast, is the road from Wainfleet to Boston (A52), past Friskney (notice the names ending in '-ey' or '-y,' denoting former islands) and Wrangle, and Old Leake, Leverton and Benington – all noble churches – and so to Boston. These are old, meandering roads from the Wolds; there are two very different roads to the west, which we shall meet in a minute or two, across the more western fens, which run straight as a die to the south.

Next to West Keal is Old Bolingbroke, birthplace of Henry IV ('Henry of Bolingbroke') in 1367. Astonishing excavations have taken place here in recent years; what were merely great, green, grassy mounds are now revealed as the walls and bulwarks and gateways of what was a royal castle till the Battle of Winceby (1643); the church is but a fragment of the beautiful church built by John of Gaunt. On the main road is the signpost 'To Mavis Enderby and Old Bolingbroke'; to this a wag once attached (according to a letter in *The Times*) a notice 'a son, both doing well'. Old Bolingbroke is a lovely spot, in a deep fold of the Wolds.

Next door again is Revesby, once the home of Sir Joseph Banks, one of Lincolnshire's greatest sons – explorer, naturalist, Fellow of the Royal Society and drainer of the Fens. The original house, of which pictures exist, was the Georgianised fragment of the monastic buildings of the Cistercian abbey (founded 1142). After his death, the property descended to his nephew, James Banks Stanhope M.P. The enormous new house was built in 1843 (by Burn) on a new and better site. This is now empty and derelict; its future is uncertain. The family have built a new house in the park. There is still the wonderful view through the lavish iron screen and beyond to the mouldering early Victorian house.

But Sir Joseph Banks is of immense importance to us as we survey this part of the county, because the new Fens here were drained by him in the years 1802–13. New Bolingbroke was the brainchild of Mr Parkinson (Joseph Banks' steward), who envisaged a great new city here; the pathetic little terraces and odd crescent of early nineteenth-century houses are due to him. It is altogether the oddest place, with Teulon's church, built in 1854. The railway and its station were added as late as 1913; alas, they are no more. Further on is the charming village of Carrington, with its chestnuts and its chapel by Jephtha Pacey, one of a number of delightful Fen chapels (see pp. 80–1). Further to the west again is another long, straight road through New York to Boston (the signpost at Coningsby points amazingly to New York and Boston); at Langrick, where the road meets the Witham, is Jephtha Pacey's finest Fen chapel (1828) with its white-painted wooden-traceried windows and short chancel. From whichever direction we approach Boston, the fantastic Stump is there to greet and overshadow us. (But for Boston itself see p. 66.)

One final and rather special attraction must be mentioned. Beyond Boston, a mile or two beyond Freiston (with its grand Benedictine priory church) the road leads towards the sea, past the turning to the North Sea Camp. A signpost points to Freiston Shore. This has its own fascination. Here was established towards the end of the eighteenth century, Lincolnshire's first seaside resort. But, alas, the sea retreated, leaving only unending mudflats, the hulk of what was once a seaside hotel, a few other houses, and its memories. For atmosphere, it should certainly be savoured.

# XII
## Highways and Byways

Such then is the County of Lincoln. The long North Sea coastline, and the great indentations of the Humber and the Wash, make it an isolated kingdom of its own, another country almost, while on the west it is cut off from Midland England by the River Trent, the Great Northern main line, and the Great North Road.

The most delightful book on the county is *Highways and Byways in Lincolnshire* by Willingham Franklin Rawnsley (Macmillan 1914) illustrated with those most romantic pencil drawings of F. L. Griggs. The highways and byways of the county are mostly very ancient. Ermine Street, which reaches Stamford from Sussex, drives a straight course through the county up to the Humber – and is, of course, a Roman road. So is the Fossway, which coming from Devon, through Bath and Leicester, enters the county between Newark and Lincoln, Tillbridge Lane is a smaller Roman road, connecting Ermine Street with Littleborough and Doncaster, crossing the Trent near Gate Burton. Many of the byways are very ancient too, and some, not so long ago, were but green lanes.

But the Romans gave us not only roads; they gave us canals too; connecting the Witham at Lincoln and the Trent at Torksey is the Roman canal called the Fossdyke, which is still extensively used. The Carr Dyke, which encompasses fifty-seven miles from Peterborough to Lincoln, is also Roman, but seems to have been formed for purposes of drainage, rather than for navigation. There are eighteenth-century waterways too, such as the Slea Navigation, which makes its way, much silted up but in process of recovery, from Sleaford (where an imposing gateway in Carre Street is entitled Navigation Wharf) to join the Witham south of Tattershall. Not far upstream, the Horncastle Navigation joins the Witham here, being a canalised section of the River Bain. Further north, the Louth Navigation makes an impressive debut in Louth itself with a grand warehouse and wharf, to make for the sea at Tetney; but alas this is much silted up. The new River Ancholme took barges for miles south from the Humber, to disembark their valuable cargo at Brandy Wharf, where the great warehouse and a welcoming public house stand solitary and somewhat forlorn beside the Navigation.

But the greatest highways ever built were of course those built in the nineteenth century – even into the twentieth – the almighty highways built for the iron horse – the railways. Rawnsley does not recommend the use of the railway to tour this enormous county; rather a tourist should have 'some form of "cycle"', or, better still, a motor car' – the 'ubiquitous motor car' he adds. Ubiquitous? That was in 1914. What would he say now? But Rawnsley was an intrepid traveller, and he writes of undertaking a walk on a winter's day from Uppingham (where he was a house master), with an undergraduate friend, to Boston – some fifty-seven miles. The walk started pleasantly enough, but as they reached the fens it began to snow, and they reached Boston trudging through four inches of snow. Dr J. Charles Cox, author of the celebrated *Little Guide to Lincolnshire*, remarks however that there is 'motoring for the wealthy tourist', but does not recommend it, on account of the temptation to 'whizz on at breathless speed, unobservant of surroundings'. This was in 1916; what would he say now? Although recommending 'walking, riding, driving or cycling', he clearly favours the railway. Every entry for the villages of Lincolnshire is prefaced by the information that it is so many miles from this station or that. The book opens with a magnificent map of Lincolnshire railways and connections. Even so, this map was not quite up to date (1916) as it does not show the new line (1913) via Coningsby and New Bolingbroke, to shorten the journey between Lincoln and Skegness.

But a remarkable map it is, with these little lines creeping to the furthest corners of the county: to Whitton in the north-west, almost on the Humber bank; to Grimsby in the north-east, at the mouth of the Humber; from Stamford in the south-west to Sutton Bridge in the south-east, hardly any tract of the great county was free from this all embracing railway network.

The Great Northern main line from King's Cross reached Grantham in 1852 (there was already a line from Grantham to Nottingham, opened in 1850), and made its way north to Newark, Retford and Doncaster. It is not always realised that the original workshops of the Great Northern Railway were at Boston, and the main line from King's Cross ran through Peterborough and Boston, and thence to Lincoln and Doncaster. This is the way Queen Victoria went to Balmoral in 1851. It is hard now to imagine those main line trains pursuing the somewhat tortuous line that until a few years ago accompanied the River Witham all the way from Boston to Lincoln, past Langrick and Tattershall, Stixwould and Bardney. The fact was that the more direct route, via Grantham, Newark and Retford (which came to be known as the Towns line), owing to the steep gradients between Peterborough and Grantham, had not been built. This did not open till 1852. Boston had two years of glory.

Until very recently there survived many of the old buildings of the Great Northern Railway workshops here at Boston. But everything is gone now. Boston is merely the end (or nearly the end) of a branch line from Grantham and Sleaford. One thing survives, and that recently and most handsomely restored, the railway station itself, with its imposing portico – an altogether delightful building as so many of these mid-nineteenth-century railway buildings are.

But even after 1852 Boston was still the centre of an important railway network, with lines to Lincoln and Grimsby to the north, to Spalding, Peterborough and London to the south, shortly to be linked to Sleaford and Grantham to the west, and to Wainfleet and Skegness to the east. The greatest trains of all, of course, went through Grantham, along the grand new Great Northern Line. It has been the author's pleasure and privilege to live for much of his life within a mile of this line, within sight of these great trains. Indeed, for several miles the line was built across the family estate, and when young he would often walk with his father to the Frinkley Lane crossing to watch the Flying Scotsman or the Queen of Scots, the Silver Jubilee (1935), or The Coronation (1937) flash by.

The other great Lincolnshire line was the East Lincolnshire Railway which ran from Grimsby to Boston, and again was one of the earliest railways in the county. There had been for some years great interest in the idea of building a line parallel with the Lincolnshire coast, and Parliament authorised the scheme in 1846. Building began at the Grimsby end in January 1847, and in September George Hussey Packe and Richard Thorold, Chairman and Vice Chairman of the Company, with other important guests travelled along the completed line to Louth. It was a journey of fourteen miles, and it took twenty minutes; the train arrived at Louth among cheering crowds and to the ringing of church bells. By 3 September 1848 the line reached Firsby, by the end of September, Boston.

The East Lincolnshire line was perhaps the most delightful of all the Lincolnshire railways: it ran from Grimsby to Louth, to Alford, and then to that all important junction, Firsby, so to Boston, and thence to Peterborough and King's Cross. Indeed, it was vintage Lincolnshire: rising as it were on the Humber bank, passing wold and marsh, and traversing fen, saluting Louth and Alford and Boston en route, it speedily reached King's Cross. Hugh Montgomery-Massingberd, then a young journalist, writes of rising betimes at Gunby, boarding the train at Burgh-le-Marsh, then addressing the British Rail breakfast grill as it approached Boston Stump, and so reaching King's Cross for a busy day in London; and returning in the evening. This splendid line, devised and built by Lincolnshire men, was ignominiously first deliberately run down, then destroyed by foreigners from London in 1970. All that survives is the little off-shoot from Boston to Wainfleet and Skegness. There were especially distinguished stations at Louth (still standing), Alford, Firsby and Boston (now restored), all, it seems, by the hand of the same architects (probably Weightman and Hadfield), and delightful branch lines to Mablethorpe and Spilsby – as well as that enchanting line from Louth through the deepest Wolds to Wragby and Bardney, and the celebrated 'loop' line from Boston to Lincoln. It is the author's great regret that he never travelled on this wonderful line; it was closed down, not without a fight, and the old track is still marked out by broken fragments. The splendid stations at Louth and Alford – now used for other purposes – still stand, the destruction of the line is now bitterly regretted.

Another remarkable line, now defunct, was the Midland and Great Northern Joint Railway. It was that rare thing; a railway that travelled east-west, not north-south. It traversed in all some two hundred miles across Norfolk, Lincolnshire and Leicestershire; on reaching Leicester, endless possibilities opened up: to Birmingham, Gloucester, Bristol, and so to the West Country. The great railway Metropolis of the M. & G. N. – its Swindon as it were – was at Melton Constable in Norfolk, more famous for its most beautiful late seventeenth-century house, home for many centuries of the Astley family.

Until only a few years ago the relics of Melton Constable

junction stood here in the middle of north-east Norfolk, but the lines – to Cromer, to Yarmouth, to Norwich, to King's Lynn – have been removed now. In earlier, happier days the lines went to all these. Here the station announcer would proclaim 'the 3.42 (or whatever it was) will depart from platform three, to Sutton Bridge, Long Sutton, Gedney, to Holbeach, to South Drove, to Counter Drain, to Bourne and beyond'. What lay beyond? Here the line, halting at the station, which was a Jacobean manor house, went on to the mysterious world beyond Bourne: Toft Tunnel, Castle Bytham, Saxby – and what else? At Castle Bytham the track became Midland – but even after 1923 the Midland and Great Northern remained independent, the trains displaying their own colours, until 1936, when all was absorbed by the L.N.E.R. Now all is silent and forlorn. The line closed in 1965, but in 1995 the name board announcing 'Gedney' still stands erect on the lonely platform. It is all forlorn and desolate now, but memories are long in Lincolnshire, and we recall with pleasure, and sorrow, that once great line, the Midland and Great Northern.

Memories of the lines are poignant, but some notable stations still stand on the surviving lines, such as that beautiful station at Sleaford, with its long platforms, and many other platforms too, beautified by barge boards and white-painted awnings. At Lincoln Central, for example, is a splendid Tudor Baronial-style station; at St Mark's, (no longer in use) a very fine neo-Classical portico. Stixwould, still surviving on the 'loop' line, has its signal box now transformed into an upstairs sitting-room, attached to the station house, with a glorious view over the Witham. Next door, at Southrey, the *Shell Guide to Lincolnshire* (1965) reported the station still open, still lit by oil lamps; in 1995 all is gone – a commentary on the near total collapse of the railways of Lincolnshire.

# XIII
## To Lincoln

When the author was a child, there were only two cars in the village. It would hardly have occurred to us to motor to Lincoln: no, the car would drive us to Caythorpe station, and we would go to the cathedral city by that delightful line which ran under the Cliff to Lincoln, through Leadenham, Navenby and Harmston – a line which was needlessly closed in 1965, though Lord Beeching had recommended its retention.

Now, with the motor car, we can drive along the Cliff (A607), through several delightful villages: Fulbeck, Leadenham, Welbourn, Wellingore, Navenby – they follow one another every mile. At Welbourn was born Field-Marshal Sir William Robertson, who rose from Private to C.I.G.S. in 1915. Here we can climb up to the Heath to discover a very special treasure: Temple Bruer. Here among the old tracks, empty roads and beech trees of the Heath, stand the precious medieval buildings of this preceptory of the Templars and Hospitallers, founded *circa* 1265. The church has gone, but one thirteenth-century tower survives. It would have been a round church, like the Temple Church in London; a part of it was standing when Samuel Buck made his print in 1726; now a grand farmhouse and buildings surround the tower. Henry VIII came here in 1538 to stay with his brother-in-law Charles Brandon, Duke of Suffolk, to whom the place had been granted at the Dissolution.

Even in the eighteenth century the Heath was so lonely and such a resort of highwaymen that Sir Francis

Dashwood of West Wycombe, and of Nocton (nearby), built the Dunston Pillar, surmounted by a lantern – 'the only land lighthouse ever raised'. After the enclosures, the Heath became safer, and a great figure of George III replaced the lantern – all ignominiously reduced in the Second World War. It should be restored to celebrate the Millennium.

At Canwick we can turn aside to see the finest of all views of the Cathedral. Alternatively, we can take the lonely Brant Road. After Brant Broughton there is no village for ten miles, and the Cathedral on its distant hill beckons to us for mile after empty mile, rather as Chartres Cathedral beckons across the flat cornfields of central France. Indeed, from all sides, Lincoln is a wonderful city to approach, whether from the north along the length of Ermine Street (A15) where the towers never seem to get any nearer, or from the east along the Witham – the view which De Wint loved to paint. It is only on entering the city that disappointment assails. Lincoln grew enormously in the nineteenth century, with the coming of the railway, and great industries grew up. Half the city is 'above hill', half 'below hill': from the top there is a view of factories and dreary streets; from the lower town there are constant glimpses of the Cathedral sailing above – and that is one of the great sights of Europe.

From the south, the long High Street leads on and on past three churches, all with distinguished early Norman or Saxon towers, over the High Bridge whose medieval vault still carries all the traffic over the Witham, with, on its west side a row of tall, sixteenth-century timbered houses, unique in England. And so we proceed to the Stonebow, the medieval gateway to the inner city, with the Guildhall above.

Those who can face the prospect can ascend on foot up Steep Hill – and steep it is – past twelfth-century and later houses, up to the Bail, and here stand in the heart of Lincoln, the Exchequergate and Cathedral facing us, the Castle at our back. Lincoln (*Lindum Colonia*), of course, is in origin a Roman city: the remarkable site on the hill with the River Witham below gave it a commanding position, the perfect situation for an important military base. Moreover, two great Roman roads, the Foss Way and Ermine Street, meet here. At the top of Bailgate, to our left, stands the Newport Arch, built in the early third century, the earliest archway in England still in everyday use. Ten years or so ago, an ill-mannered lorry, passing this way, did its best to knock it down, but came off by far the worse in the struggle. Newport Arch was the North gate. The foundations and fragments of the East gate, with fragments of the Roman wall, are visible by the Eastgate Hotel; portions of the West gate are embedded in the Castle mound, while remains of the South gate can be seen in houses on the Steep. In the little garden on the site of the small Victorian church of St Paul are the recently excavated foundations of the earliest Christian church in the city: the basilica of St Paul, with its eastern apse, here in the middle of what was once the forum.

But as we stand here it is medieval Lincoln which surrounds us. Behind, stands the fourteenth-century gate to the Castle, which was built in 1068 by William the Conqueror. Here, in the south-west corner of the Roman *castrum*, in front of us, stands one of the greatest Gothic churches in the world.

Lincoln Cathedral is a giant; everything nearby – the houses of Minster Yard, the gateways – is dominated by its stupendous presence. The visitor will stand before its great West front, walk around the exterior, examine towers, pinnacles, transepts, flying buttresses. Inside, awestruck, he will observe the arcades, the traceried windows, the medieval woodwork, the ancient stained glass, the vast spaces.

The See of Lincoln was founded in 1072, transferred here from Dorchester-on-Thames. Remigius, the first Norman to be given an English bishopric, became first Bishop of Lincoln and the diocese stretched from the Humber to the Thames. There was a Saxon minster on the hill, but this was pulled down to build Remigius' new cathedral. All that remains of this is the façade of the West front, and the lower part of the West towers. In an earthquake in 1141 a great part of Remigius' cathedral collapsed.

St Hugh, who became Bishop of Lincoln in 1192, was the founder of the new Early English cathedral. He began building the East end, moving down to the choir, then to the crossing and the nave, to join up with the Norman West front. Following French practice, the East end terminated in an apse with radiating chapels. In the middle of the next century this was pulled down and, in its place, the celebrated Angel Choir was built in the Geometrical Decorated style to enlarge and enhance the cathedral, and to provide a setting for the shrine of St Hugh. This is the cathedral which we see today. It was completed in 1280; with its sumptuous carvings and delicate tracery it must constitute one of the most splendid examples of the Decorated period in England.

Standing before the West front, it is easy to distinguish the Norman West porch with its round arches from the lofty Gothic screen which was built above and around it. In the Norman façade the remarkable sculptured frieze will be noted; it has much in common with similar work at St Denis Abbey near Paris, and with the frieze on the façade of Modena Cathedral in Italy. The large windows are, of course, Perpendicular insertions, while from behind the Gothic screen rise the two Norman towers, to which the tall upper storeys were added at the end of the fourteenth century.

The nave belongs to the first half of the thirteenth century; the bays are wide – typically English – and the triforium has broad low openings. The vaulting has a complex, palm-like pattern of ribs. Into the great transept could be fitted both nave and chancel of an ordinary sized cathedral. The rose window in the north transept – the Dean's Eye – contains glass made for it between 1200 and 1220; the Bishop's Eye in the south transept, with its flamboyant tracery, contains a medley of ancient fragments assembled here with consummate skill in the eighteenth century. Beneath this is the seated figure of the saintly Bishop King (Bishop of Lincoln 1885–1910) by Sir William Richmond – Bishop King, beloved and revered.

St Hugh's Choir and the narrow eastern transepts were built at the very end of the twelfth century; there are curious, almost experimental features here, such as the odd lopsided vaulting of the choir. The stalls, with their profusion of pinnacles and wealth of carved misericords, must rank with Carlisle, Chester and Ripon as the finest medieval stalls in England.

The Chapter House belongs to the middle of the thirteenth century, and, next to Worcester, is the earliest of the specifically English octagonal chapter houses built round a central pillar. The Victorian glass darkens this splendid interior; the exterior is graceful with its array of flying buttresses. Nearby is the statue of Lord Tennyson, born at Somersby in this county, with his hat and his dog. It is by G. F. Watts, 1905.

The cloister is a luxury in a non-monastic cathedral (as was Lincoln); it is a pleasure to walk round it, enjoying the majestic views of towers and chancel and transepts. Here, too, is the final pleasure of the Cathedral: Wren's Library, built for Dean Honywood in 1674, raised on an almost Italianate loggia, with bay trees grown in tubs under the arcade. 'I have always held,' wrote Ruskin, 'and am prepared against all comers to maintain, that the Cathedral of Lincoln is out and out the most precious piece of architecture in the British Isles, and, roughly speaking, worth any other two Cathedrals we have.'

# XIV
# To the other Towns of Lincolnshire

Few appreciate how enormous the County of Lincoln is, how vast the spaces, how great the distances. My father, who spent much of his childhood here a century ago, had a happy Lincolnshire childhood in the 1880s and early 1890s, but it was a childhood constricted by the distances which could be covered by a carriage and pair, or by a dog cart. To travel further, even to get to Lincoln, or to go away to school or to Oxford, it was essential to take the train – and at the end of the last century the railways were still a novelty.

Thirty or so years later, my father who had spent a long life in the army and travelled across the world in the service of king and country, had never yet been to Louth. So he and my mother decided that we should all celebrate their silver wedding (in 1938) by motoring over to Louth, exploring a little of the Lincolnshire Wolds and having a picnic lunch on a still remote stretch of the Lincolnshire seashore. On our way home we stopped for a wonderfully old-fashioned Lincolnshire tea at the Rodney Hotel in Horncastle. My father was nearly sixty and this was his first visit to this remote and enchanted part of Lincolnshire. Sixty or more years later, this part of the county still seems remote and enchanted; the railways have come and gone; the motor car is still ubiquitous (as it was to the author of *Highways and Byways*), but mile after endless mile of Lincolnshire wolds and marsh, even in 1995, remains remote and unconquered.

Let us now visit some of the towns of Lincolnshire.

There are many ways to approach Louth, but the best of

all is to take the road from Wragby, past Hainton and Burgh-on-Bain, Grimblethorpe and Welton-le-Wold. Suddenly in the distance that sublime spire comes in sight: suddenly the wolds part, to reveal it at the end of a gently sloping fold in the hills – it marks the town which is the capital of its countryside. Then we pass Thorpe Hall, turn the last corner past the handgate on to Hubberts Hills, and into Westgate. There can be few fairer entries, and few fairer towns to enter. First comes a lovable little row of smaller eighteenth-century houses, all different, each with steps with iron hand rails up to its front door; then past Irish Hill to the finest house in the town, The Mansion, with all the graciousness of the age of William and Mary, for many years the home of Jack Yates, that much loved bookseller and joint author of the *Shell Guide to Lincolnshire*. Breakneck Lane, so well named, leads off to the right, and then follows a whole procession of lovely houses on either side; of special charm is Westgate House, with its early nineteenth-century, wide bow windows, erected on low Doric columns, and a horseshoe staircase leading up to the front door; it was the town house of the Chaplins of Tathwell. But the whole of Westgate is a delight – leading up to the west front of the Parish Church. This is a breathtaking sight.

Louth spire rises up, stage after stage of almost impossible beauty, to the enormous pinnacles which support the spire itself, with flying buttresses made, it would seem, of lace. The spire is the latest of all English medieval spires, having been built two hundred years after Grantham, which was the earliest. It was begun in 1501, and completed in 1515 at a cost of £307 7s 5d. It is a thrill to stand under the tower, which with its great windows rises like a lantern. The church itself is a little earlier in date, and though wide and spacious (like all the great churches of the Marsh), it is in some ways disappointing; the meagre Victorian furnishings – in wood, stone and marble, by

James Fowler – make the interior seem empty, and the proportions of this grand barn are unhappy too.

Beyond the church, Mercer Row leads into the Market Place, with good houses and shops all around. The one with the glorious bulging window was Jack Yates' bookshop; next door is a great stucco terrace, with Corinthian pilasters, like a Regency terrace in Brighton; opposite, Parkers' the printers had the distinction of printing Tennyson's first volume of poetry, *Poems, by Two Brothers* (1827). Nearby is the incredible Market Hall, in red brick Byzantine Gothic, with its narrow clock tower and spirelet, while behind us stands another fascinating building, the Town Hall of 1853 (by Pearson Bellamy), whose front has been described as looking like an annexe to the Vatican, its back like a slaughter house.

But there are lovely houses in every street in Louth. Suffice to mention Bridge Street Terrace, a most handsome, tall pedimented brick terrace of *circa* 1825 and, just over the bridge, the old Mill of 1755. It is a town glowing with old red tiles and old red brick; it has wonderfully preserved itself, and a visit now, in the late twentieth century, is a tonic.

A visit to Horncastle is also a tonic. It is a smaller town, and altogether less grand, but it is a place of great charm. Driving in from Woodhall Spa, the Wolds open out, and there in the little valley, where the Rivers Bain and Waring meet, is Horncastle, like Louth, aglow with old red tiles and old red brick. Drive down West Street; there is nothing remarkable, only a very pleasing street of warm brick houses and cottages. Over the Bain, and we are in the Market Place. Perhaps it is market day, and stalls and shoppers abound; in the middle is the Victorian statue of Edward Stanhope of Revesby, Secretary of State for War (1893). Nearby, in High Street, is the big square Georgian house, now a butcher's shop, which was Sir Joseph Banks' town house; the Stanhopes inherited Revesby from Banks. High Street leads into the Bull Ring, and all around are old shops or public houses. North Street has several stylish houses, and at the top is the imposing Court House of white brick and stone (1865) to close the vista – now ignominiously renamed 'Job Centre'. South Street and East Street have still more charming small houses (especially East Street), and the Parish Church, and its little square near the Market Place, is delightful too, built in the local greenstone (Early English and Decorated), with its squat tower and candle snuffer spirelet. Here we can overlook the Waring, flowing by.

Horncastle – as its name suggests, was a Roman town, and its *Castrum* formed roughly a parallelogram between the two rivers. Fragments of its walls and foundations survive.

Caistor, as its name suggests, is also a Roman town. Built in the sloping hillside of the western escarpment of the Wolds, its position was, of course, of considerable importance to the Romans. But, as at Horncastle, only fragments or foundations of the Roman walls survive; a very loose parallelogram seems to have formed the *Castrum*. Caistor is an attractive little town, with its medieval Parish Church, its seventeenth-century Grammar School, its spacious Market Square and accompanying streets; there are no buildings of any special importance, but like so many of the smaller towns of Lincolnshire it has considerable charm.

Spilsby, lying east-west along the top of the Wold, the centre marked out by the imposing tower of the medieval (but Victorianised) Parish Church, is of special charm. The Market Place is a long parallelogram, with Sir John Franklin to survey it, and The White Hart occupying its western corner so completely. Opposite the Parish Church is the splendid early nineteenth-century Court House, with its grand portico (by H. E. Kendall) of 1824. But the great thrill is the long avenue which leads down from just west of the church to Eresby. It is now broken in the middle by the new by-pass road, but (all the same) goes on and on straight to the site of Eresby House. The great house was burnt in 1769; there remains one sumptuous gatepier, crowned with a great urn, and a few fragmentary buildings. The family never rebuilt, merely transferred all to Grimsthorpe, where Vanbrugh had recently added his tremendous extension to the medieval and Tudor buildings there. So the monuments at Spilsby stop abruptly – to be continued in still greater magnificence at Edenham. But Spilsby and Eresby remain enchanting.

A visit to Sleaford is always a pleasure: to arrive at the railway station and admire its long platforms alongside the road, their elegant white-painted canopies, sky lights, windows, the passenger bridge, the stone Tudor station house of 1859, the splendid brick Victorian warehouses behind. The whole station makes a delightful composition. Beyond the level crossing, turning into Southgate, is the 1920s Picture Drome with its little Art Deco dome, the cinema still in operation (1995). Southgate leads up to the Handley Monument, a grand Gothic memorial to Henry Handley M.P. (1850), and so across a little stream of the Slea into the Market Place, a charming square, presided over by the west front of the Parish Church, with its very early broach spire, and wonderful traceried Decorated windows. The exterior of Sleaford church is without question magnificent, with its very early spire (late twelfth-early thirteenth-century), its very rich west front, its great array of pinnacles, and, above all, the glorious and enormous curvilinear traceried windows, with the Perpendicular windows of the clerestory above, and the Perpendicular chancel. Inside, there is no disappointment. The medieval rood screen ('the most perfect in England' according to Pugin), with the rood itself and figures by Comper, and the remarkable series of tombs and monuments to the Carre family, Sleaford's great sixteenth-seventeenth-century benefactors, are all breathtaking.

Opposite is Carre's Hospital, founded in 1636 by the Carre family and rebuilt by H. E. Kendall in 1830. It is a pleasure to stand in its open courtyard and survey the superb traceried windows of the nave. Nearby, down Carre Street is the almost Egyptian portico inscribed 'Navigation Office 1792'. Here was the wharf of the Slea Navigation (see p. 51); the little River Slea was canalised to join the Witham near Tattershall. After languishing for a century, it is now being restored, and we can go up Eastgate to visit the eighteenth-century Cogglesford Mill and the Navigation en route.

But the centre of Sleaford, with its stone houses, is all a delight: the Sessions House with its restrained Gothic façade by H. E. Kendall (1831) faces the west front of the church; opposite, the old Bristol Arms is now, alas, a shopping arcade. It used to be a delightful, old-fashioned hotel, unselfconsciously furnished with good things, and many old prints of Lincolnshire. In the region of Westgate are some unexpected corners with little houses and their gardens approached each by its bridge over the stream. To the south of the town, dominating the skyline, stands the magnificent Maltings built at the very end of the last century, a most impressive monument to Victorian prosperity and the importance of the hop.

There is a grandeur about Boston which sets it apart from other country towns in Lincolnshire; a grandeur which is reflected in the grandeur of the Stump, the loftiest medieval tower in England. Boston, in its time, was the second port in England; for a long time the first. The prodigious Parish Church is a reminder of this. Stand on the Town Bridge and look upstream: the view of the great church is unforgettable, with its mammoth tower, two hundred and seventy-two feet high, standing on the very bank of the river. Or turn into the Market Place, and see the chancel, elegant and enormous, projecting into the very centre of the town. It is, in the words of Doctor J. Charles Cox, 'the largest and most impressive parish church in England'. It dominates the town; it dominates the countryside. The church is Decorated, the tower Perpendicular, and the scale of everything is tremendous. Inside, the eye is carried on up to the East end with its sixty-four medieval stalls in the chancel, crowned with nineteenth-century canopies, and splendid Victorian reredos. There is a whole range of monuments of every period; a Jacobean pulpit, and important east window by W. H. O'Connor. The only jarring note in this incredible interior, is the recent, hideous nave altar and accompanying furniture.

Boston is Botolph's town; here in 654, St Botolph founded a monastery, which was destroyed by the Danes. The first charter was granted by King John in 1204, and the years that followed were years of great prosperity, with trade between Boston and Flanders booming. The tide turned, the port of Boston became silted up, trade declined, and the discovery of America brought trade to Bristol. In the sixteenth century Boston became almost a 'distressed' area. Recovery was slow. The seventeenth century saw the great emigration to North American of Puritans and Pilgrim Fathers; the Mayflower sailed in 1620 (from North Killingholme), and seven further ships in 1630 – with such a preponderance of Boston families that they gave their name to the capital of Massachusetts. In 1633 John Cotton – the celebrated 'preaching' Vicar of Boston, who would often detain a congregation for five hours in church – departed, together with Bellingham, the Recorder of Boston, destined to become Governor of Massachusetts.

In the eighteenth and nineteenth centuries great works were performed, dredging the Haven and making new channels and docks, and straightening the course of the Witham. Trade has returned. Boston once again flourishes.

The Market Place is a long, pleasantly irregular space, dominated (as has been said) by the church. There are other impressive buildings, too, such as William Atkinson's Assembly Rooms (1822), and William Lumby's Corporation Building (1772); and South Street leads to the best buildings in Boston: Shodfriars Hall (sixteenth century, restored by by Oldrid Scott), the Old Guildhall (fifteenth century), and down Spain Lane, the thirteenth-century refectory of the Dominican Friary. Next to the Guildhall is Boston's most distinguished mansion, Fydell House (c. 1726), once the house of the Fydell family, wine merchants, whose beautiful eighteenth- and early nineteenth-century monuments are in the church. Opposite, in South Square, are some of the grand warehouses, so splendid a feature of Boston – and, then: disaster!

It is difficult to describe the damage done to the town by what is called John Adams Way, a monstrous dual carriageway, which makes its slithery way from the Bargate to the Haven Bridge, and on beyond the river. A dual carriageway through the very heart of this ancient town! The very bowels of Boston are here cut out; the traffic passes through between what appears to be a series of bomb-sites. Not only is this a disaster; the ancient High Street, the other side of the river, is badly damaged too. A twee notice, 'High Street', leads down a dismal street of once distinguished eighteenth-century houses, some boarded up, all now depressed. Mercifully, the intriguing early eighteenth-century terrace, at the far end (popularly called the Barracks, which it never was), survives. But it is a sad street now. There are a few stranded Georgian houses beyond, and a special reward, in Skirbeck Quarter, the intimate and beautiful church of St Thomas by Temple Moore (1912ff).

In the docks there is all the fascination and excitement of masts and funnels and cranes; the railway station (*circa*

1848) has been beautifully restored (see also pp. 52), and the magnificent Maud Foster windmill (1819) presides over the Maud Foster drain – in full working order. Further to the north there are delightful Victorian houses and terraces in the Spilsby Road – some quite grand. So all is not lost. And wherever we go in this ancient and distinguished borough, the almost incredible Stump is there too, sailing above us.

It is the Welland that gives Spalding its character, and from early times brought in its trade. The river, in a deep tidal channel, runs through the town like a street, and it is a pleasure to walk upstream and then downstream along its banks – which are in themselves dignified streets of delightful houses and terraces. The town grew up originally round the important Benedictine priory founded *circa* 1087, and the river brought trade and wealth from early times: the export of corn and potatoes, the import of timber and coal. The parish church was founded in the late thirteenth century (as we know from contemporary records) under the aegis of the priory, and the town grew. The priory was dissolved in 1536, but we can get a glimpse of an unusually cultivated little town in the eighteenth century, when Maurice Johnson and his friends founded the Spalding Gentlemen's Society in 1710. Two or three of them, such as Newton and Stukeley, had close local connections, but others such as Pope, Addison and Sloane must have come regularly from London. It is a pleasure that so much of this little eighteenth-century town survives.

If we start in the Market Place we can do an enjoyable tour of the town. There are few major blots in Spalding; one of them is here, in the Market Place: the appalling monster called the 'South Holland Centre'. What does this word 'Centre' mean? What is it the 'Centre' of? Whoever can have imposed this brutal building on beautiful, intimate Spalding?

We cross the town bridge and turn right into Church Gate, and here is another blot: a perfectly absurd new road to the west end of the parish church called 'The Vista'. 'The Vista'? No medieval church was intended to be approached head-on. Look at Louth, look at Grantham, those two remarkable spires were intended to be – and are – approached obliquely. The correct approach to Spalding Church is from Church Street, across the churchyard, to the north porch. May 'The Vista' be obliterated!

But we were in Church Gate. Here stands that remarkable house, Ayscoughfee Hall, in origin a Tudor house, now amazingly encrusted with early nineteenth-century, sugary adornments; in all a glorious piece of confectionery. It was the house of Maurice Johnson and of several generations of his family. We can proceed down this delightful street, all the time looking at the attractive terraces across the river, then cross the bridge, and repeat the pleasure from the other side.

If we go down Double Street we can repeat the process along this stretch of the river, passing a number of good eighteenth-century houses, and one of the few seventeenth-century houses in Spalding, Willesby Hall, with its gables and mullioned windows. At the end we can cross the river again, and return on the other side, admiring the larger houses here, especially Holland House, by the Spalding architect William Sands (1768). These were houses indeed for members of the Gentlemen's Society.

And so, down Church Street to the Parish Church, to be viewed here to perfection, a wonderful medieval composition, with spire at the south-west corner and porch of two storeys close at hand. This is Perpendicular, with a fan vault within. There are Perpendicular windows in the north aisle and transept; next comes Sir George Gilbert Scott's north chancel chapel, then the Early English chancel beyond. This is how to view a medieval church. It is glorious within, almost as wide as it is long, with double nave aisles, lancets in the chancel, and many monuments and hatchments of the Johnson family of Ayscoughfee Hall. This is the heart of Spalding, and it is delightful.

Gainsborough is really a very unusual little town, in no way like any other Lincolnshire town. It stands on the Lincolnshire bank of the River Trent and there is a handsome eighteenth-century bridge (by William Weston, 1787) to lead us over into Nottinghamshire, if we wish. We can inspect the river from here – then make our way into the middle of the town.

Along the River Trent here are the quays, where, as George Eliot has described them in *The Mill on the Floss*, 'black ships laden with fresh scented fir planks, with rounded sacks of oil bearing seed, or with the dark glitter of coal' have always tied up; here too, stand the great warehouses (some of eighteenth-century date), where the imports of this inland port are housed. The many narrow streets in this part of the town lead us past great warehouses and forbidding factories – and suddenly, almost by accident, there appear the tall Tudor chimneys and towers of the Old Hall, one of the most important surviving ancient manor houses in England. It stands on a drab patch of grass, surrounded by depressing nineteenth-century semi-detached villas. Its survival here is amazing.

This grand fifteenth-century house, built of brick and timber – only the great Hall oriel window is of stone – was in origin the seat of Lord Burgh, then of the Hickmans, baronets, originally London merchants, but related to the Burghs. In the eighteenth century they moved out to the 'sylvan pleasances' of Thonock (to the north-east). In the course of the next century or two, different parts of the house were used as a linen factory, a theatre, a Congregational chapel, a public house, a corn exchange and a block of tenements. All the Hickman property descended to the Bacons (premier Baronets of England), and in 1952 Sir

Edmund Bacon leased it, at a peppercorn rent, to the Friends of the Old Hall Association, who began repairs. It is now administered by the County Council, and open to the public.

Nearby stands the distinguished eighteenth-century Parish Church, built in 1736ff by Francis Smith of Warwick, and attached to the Perpendicular tower of the earlier church. It is a most handsome exterior, with its giant pilasters supporting its cornice and entablature, then a balustraded parapet. It is a grand spacious classical interior, with Corinthian columns and galleries, all beautifully decorated.

Gainsborough is an ancient place, for all the streets of red brick nineteenth-century housing. The historic Old Hall and the grand eighteenth-century church testify to its long established importance, an importance which has always been due to the great river.

In 1963, *Country Life* published three scholarly articles by Arthur Oswald on Grantham, in their excellent 'Old Towns Revisited' series. In the last thirty years so much of the middle of the town has been wantonly destroyed that it is hard to think of anybody wanting to write such articles now; indeed, to drive through High Street or Watergate or Vine Street is very depressing. In Watergate, one of the principal entries to the town, one whole side of the street has been replaced by a miserable car-park, a few old houses having been allowed to remain on the other side. In Vine Street, the mysterious, curving entry leading to the parish church has gone, replaced by the quite unworthy so-called Watergate House, simultaneously disfiguring all three streets with its rounded façade. True, the celebrated medieval Angel Hotel and the eighteenth-century front of The George have been allowed to survive, but The George, described fifty years ago as 'the best hotel on the Great North Road', has now been converted into a shopping arcade, full of empty shops. Further down the street, the sacrifice of decent Georgian houses continues; most recently Waterloo House has been replaced by a barbarous block, quite unsuited to a country town. But pride of place for brutishness must go to the new General Post Office (1968). This dominating concrete monster would no doubt look well enough in Slough, but in historic Grantham, it is a nightmare. Are our 'planners' and 'developers' really so insensitive, so ignorant? It is very disturbing that all this has been *allowed* to happen.

It is still possible to walk round the town without seeing these major horrors. Drive in from Manthorpe; very soon the scene is dominated by the great medieval spire, towering over everything around. Drive on down Castlegate, by the King's School, and the street passes the east end of the church with its triple gables and huge traceried windows, and, opposite, the stables and garden wall of Grantham House. On down the street past The Beehive Inn with its living sign – a real beehive in a lime tree growing in the gutter – to St Peter's Hill. Here on the green stands the statue (by Theed) of Sir Isaac Newton (see p. 34), and behind him the Victorian Guildhall (by William Watkins, 1864), built, says *Kelly's Directory*, 'in a mixed Renaissance style'. Further on, down the London Road, and round the station, are the results of nineteenth-century industrialisation. Ruston and Hornby's great engineering works were established here as early as 1815, the railway arrived (from Nottingham) in 1850, and the main line to London and Edinburgh in 1852 (see p. 52).

Westgate, which leads to the station, is one of the least spoiled of Grantham's streets. Broad at that end, it narrows as it winds towards the Market Place. And from there there is a view of the façade of the celebrated Angel Hotel, one of the finest medieval inns in England. The wide pointed Gothic gateway leads into the yard behind, and the central window rests on a gilded corbel of an angel. This wonderful front is late fifteenth-century; there are charming rooms inside, and the bay windows are crowned with low, stone vaults, all of considerable beauty. Behind, there is a tall eighteenth-century brick terrace, built to accommodate travellers of a later age; we can walk past here on our way to the church.

The existence of this ancient hostelry and the existence of this superb medieval church point to the importance of Grantham in the Middle Ages. Not only is the spire of great beauty, the whole west front is a medieval masterpiece, with the enormous geometrical windows on either side. Here Ruskin stood spellbound. The spire soars above us, two hundred and eighty-one feet high, built between 1230 and 1300, before Salisbury (404ft), before Norwich (345ft), before Coventry (300ft), before Louth (294ft). In its day it was the loftiest spire in England. Walk round the exterior and absorb the wonderful traceried windows which continue all round. Come inside; the church is enormously wide, with aisles almost as broad as the nave, divided by early thirteenth-century arcades. The power of this remarkable interior is horizontal rather than vertical. There is a fourteenth-century crypt, an interesting collection of monuments and splendid Victorian furnishings.

The setting of the church is perfect, with a good-looking eighteenth-century rectory. Next to this is the King's School, mentioned already which was founded in 1528 by Bishop Fox of Winchester; with its original little quad and hall, rather reminiscent of a small Oxford college, it is a building of great charm. Grantham House at the east end of the church is in origin fourteenth-century, the home of the Hall family. Later, it was used as the dower house to Belton, and was delightfully Georgianised. It was given to the National Trust in 1944 and is open to the public at certain times.

On our way out of the town we can take the old Great North Road, by North Parade. Here there is a long terrace of small late-Georgian houses; these were known as the Bachelors' Houses, which bachelors could rent for the hunting season and keep their horses in what was an open meadow opposite, reminding us of the importance of the Belvoir Hunt hereabouts. And at the corner with Broad Street was the famous grocer's shop, where a future prime minister was born in 1925.

Bourne is an ancient little town on the edge of the Fens, the reputed birthplace of Hereward the Wake and the birthplace of William Cecil, Lord Burghley. The road from Grantham passes Vanbrugh's Grimsthorpe, passes Edenham Church, meets the road from Stamford, and descends. The little town looks charming, presided over by its abbey, and on entering the discerning visitor will be taken with the very attractive grand Victorian (or Edwardian) villas which greet him. But the whole of this street is delightful, with the trim white Baptist Chapel (1835) and pleasant shops. And so to the Market Place, presided over so ceremoniously by Bryan Browning's Town Hall (1821). Nearby, The Angel Hotel with its pretty barge boards and, appropriately, The Burghley Arms, look on. North Street is delightful, with equally pleasant shops and Victorian villas, but a short distance to the south, South Street and Abbey Road lead to the abbey. The Bourne stream accompanies this quiet cul-de-sac, a little cast iron bridge leads to a pretty house opposite, with mullioned windows, set in its river-side gardens – and the abbey is before us.

Bourne Abbey was founded in 1138 for Arrosian Canons (a branch of the Augustinians). It was neither large nor wealthy, and the uncompleted west front testifies to this; the Norman nave, never replaced, does so also. It is a lovely church. Nothing remains of the monastic buildings, and a large bowling green now occupies the site of the cloisters. There were nine canons at the time of the Dissolution.

75

Not far away is the Red Hall, sixteenth-century, gabled home of the Digby family, but in the nineteenth century converted to serve as the railway station on the Midland and Great Northern Joint Railway! It sounds ridiculous, but little harm was done, and a very handsome station it made. With the closure of the railway, it has become an impressive museum, with delightful meeting rooms adjoining.

Stamford is unquestionably one of the most beautiful towns in England. It is the perfect size, and built of the most glorious local stone. It has five ancient churches, and one of the greatest of all great houses at its gate, fine streets, intimate lanes, very good hotels, decent shops, handsome houses in every street, and the River Welland running through; with two railway stations (one, alas, no longer functioning) what more could be desired?

Stamford is not a Roman town, but with Casterton to the north and Castor to the south, the ford over the Welland must have been used by the Romans. Ermine Street passed nearby, the Normans built a castle, and fragments of the ancient walls survive.

The town had three great periods of prosperity; the first was medieval and religious, when the earlier churches were built, and many religious orders came here to found houses, colleges and schools. The second was commercial, when great wealth came to the town from wool and cloth, and the Perpendicular churches were built by the wealthy wool merchants. This prosperity continued into the sixteenth century, when Queen Elizabeth gave the manor to William Cecil, Lord Burghley, and it is to his descendants that we owe an incalculable debt for the protection of this superlative town. In the eighteenth century, with the increase of traffic on the Great North Road, Stamford became a great halting place for travellers, and the inns and hotels flourished. Moreover, it became a great centre of social life for the neighbourhood, the local aristocracy and gentry patronised assembly rooms and theatre, and their elegant houses in every street are a lasting memorial to their good taste and learning.

The best way to see Stamford must be to enter from the south, past the Bottle Lodges, to Burghley and into High Street St Martin's. This is the view that Scott loved and Turner painted; there can be no more splendid an entry to any town in England. St Martin's Church with its bold Perpendicular tower greets us; opposite is The George Hotel, with its sign crossing the road, and its splendid rooms, delicious food and enchanting walled garden. We cross the bridge: the eighteenth-century town hall comes first, then the full glory of St Mary's bursts upon us – the finest broach spire in England. Beautiful houses surround it; in St Mary's Place with its cobbles; and onwards in St Mary's Street, into St George's Square, with St George's Church on one side, theatre and assembly rooms on the other. This is all a most delightful little corner of the town.

But turning back again towards St Mary's, and turning right at the end of St Mary's Street, we come to Red Lion Square, dominated by All Saints' Church, but with St John's at one side also, at the corner of the High Street. Broad Street turns off to the right, parallel with High Street and leads to Browne's Hospital; St Paul's Street follows (round the corner) leading to Stamford School, and the Brasenose Gate. There is a replica knocker now; the original was returned to Brasenose College, Oxford last century; it was stolen and brought to Stamford when members of the University of Oxford migrated to Stamford in the fourteenth century to set up a rival Brasenose College. They were obliged to return to their alma mater. But we must retrace our steps – this time through High Street, pedestrianised, but with many useful shops – back into Red Lion Square. Behind All Saints' a narrow entry leads into the most enchanting street of all, Barn Hill. Here it is a case of one beautiful house after another, some small, some grand, one very grand. No. 6 has an eighteenth-century bay window with Gothick glazing bars and splendid plaster-work and panelling inside. Next is Barn Hill House, very grand with its three-storeyed frontispiece standing back in a spacious setting from the street. It is in origin seventeenth-century, but has become increasingly grand by degrees. A little further up is Stukeley House, on the site of the house where Dr Stukeley lived. One of the founders of the Spalding Gentlemen's Society and of the Society of Antiquaries, Stukeley lived in Barn Hill as Rector of All Saints' (1729–47). And so farewell – down the narrow hill to Scotgate and away.

Lincoln on its hill: Samuel and Nathaniel Buck's prospect (1743) of the Cathedral across the River Witham.

Osgodby: the earliest Roman Catholic church in Lincolnshire (1793). *Peter Burton/Harland Walshaw*

Frithville: one of Jephtha Pacey's little fen chapels (1821). *Peter Burton/Harland Walshaw*

Algarkirk: a grand Decorated window in the south transept of this superb cruciform fenland church. *Peter Burton/Harland Walshaw*

Stamford: Barn Hill leads down to All Saints church, with St Mary's beyond. *Peter Burton/Harland Walshaw*

A fenland dyke near Crowland. *Peter Burton/Harland Walshaw*

A remote Wold hamlet: Haugham, near Louth, with the church by C. Willoughby and W. A. Nicholson, 1840. *Peter Burton/Harland Walshaw*

Gate Burton: The little temple surveying the River Trent, known as 'The Burton Shatoo'. John Platt, architect, 1748. *Peter Burton/Harland Walshaw*

Well Vale: the house built *c*. 1725 for James Bateman, from the portico of the church and aligned on the front door of the house. *Peter Burton/Harland Walshaw*

Gibraltar Point, on the northern shore of the Wash.
*Peter Burton/Harland Walshaw*

Grimsthorpe Castle: Sir John Vanbrugh's north front, built for the 2nd Duke of Ancaster, *c*. 1725. *Peter Burton/Harland Walshaw*

Alford railway station, on the old East Lincolnshire Railway, 1848. *Peter Burton/Harland Walshaw*

Harlaxton Manor: the lower vestibule and staircase leading up to the baroque glories above. *Peter Burton/Harland Walshaw*

Kirton-in-Holland: the figure of William Dennis by P. Lindsey Clark (1930) presides in front of the Town Hall. *Peter Burton/Harland Walshaw*

Old Woodhall: the Wellington Monument, erected by Colonel Elmhirst of West Ashby, against the background of oaks, planted from acorns, and sown immediately after the Battle of Waterloo. *Peter Burton/Harland Walshaw*

The Royal Air Force College, Cranwell, built 1929-33, and designed by Sir James Grey West. *Peter Burton/Harland Walshaw*

# XV
# A Collection of Country Churches

'But you've left out Amber Hill,' said an old friend, soon after the publication of 'Lincolnshire Churches Revisited' (Michael Russell, 1989): 'it's a delightful book, but you've left out Amber Hill.'

The author stood rebuked. Six hundred and more Lincolnshire churches, all in their proper places in the Gazetteer, but no Amber Hill; he had never been there; how could he revisit it? So to the map and the directories; an exhaustive search revealed Amber Hill on the map, at the very end of a minor road in Holland Fen, where the road petered out into the fen; 'Amber Hill,' he read in *Kelly's Directory* (1937), 'a gravel field of thirty acres, and extra parochial ... St John Baptist, Chapel of Ease to Holland Fen was erected in 1867; there are three hundred sittings.' 'A gravel field' – hence Amber Hill. Those who know the Lincolnshire fens will appreciate the meaning of 'hill' in this context: Gedney Hill comes to mind, Chapel Hill, and above all others, those signposts near Weston St Mary: 'To Weston Hills'. Weston Hills, comparable perhaps to the Malverns? No, 'hill' around here means perhaps six inches above flood level. After all, everything is comparative.

And so to Amber Hill itself – to make reparation for its omission in the past. There it was, at the very end of this minor fen road, just as it petered out on its way to nowhere: a little red-brick Victorian church with a bellcote at the west end, an apse at the east, designed by Edward Browning of Stamford, and built in 1867 at the expense of the Revd Prebendary Basil Beridge of Algarkirk. The same partnership is to be found not far away at Fosdyke, close to the mouth of the Welland, where the much larger, indeed very grand new church was designed by the same architect again at the sole cost of Prebendary Beridge of Algarkirk. At Fosdyke there is some village; at Amber Hill but a cottage or two, a village settlement perhaps a mile away. 'There are three hundred sittings,' remarks Kelly. When did three hundred last kneel together at Amber Hill? The bleak landscape here is perhaps an acquired taste; enormous fields, no trees, scarcely any hedges, the few buildings crouching close to the black soil; 'intersected' says Kelly 'by several drains'. Exactly.

Not so far away are those most lately drained fens, drained between 1802 and 1813 under Sir Joseph Banks and John Rennie: East Fen, West Fen, and Wildmore Fen. 'These lands', wrote William White (1842), 'were a few years ago a watery morass, and had neither house nor inhabitant, but are now fertile, and have drains which are navigable to Boston and other places.' Some forty thousand acres in all were drained. Long, straight roads cross these fens; imagine Sir Joseph driving from Revesby, south to Boston, on that long straight road through New Boling-broke and Carrington. New Bolingbroke, as we have seen, was the creation of his steward John Parkinson, who planned a new city here; all that was achieved was an odd little line of terraces and a crescent; it was he who by accident founded Woodhall Spa. Boring for coal he discovered only important mineral water. He died, poor man, bankrupt. Carrington is much the most attractive of the new fen villages, thanks to generous planting of splendid trees along the road. It is named after the first Lord Carrington, owner of the soil, and ancestor of the present peer, the former Foreign Secretary. There are good early nineteenth-century houses, and the first of the little fen chapels designed by Jephtha Pacey. These were sanctioned by Act of Parliament in 1826 and Carrington Church was the first to be built. It is altogether charming, as are all the other five: Medville, Frithville, Langrick, Wildmore and (slightly later and grander, and by another hand) Eastville. They are in fact little Georgian boxes, with overhanging eaves, pointed windows, and little Georgian cupolas, all the woodwork painted white. They are absolutely charming, and indeed unique.

Of course Holland is one of the three Parts of Lincoln-shire – the others being Lindsey and Kesteven – famed for the finest of all our churches, perhaps the greatest collection anywhere of glorious medieval churches. It may seem odd to extol these humble little fen chapels. But go and look at them: they are irresistible.

## The Churches of Holland

But the great churches of Holland; where do we begin, and indeed where do we end? It is an unending procession: we meet them, one after another, as we travel through the long roads of the fens. Here in Holland are the finest churches in the county, and some of the finest in all England, a fact which has always foxed archaeologists, since there is no local building stone at all, and instead of bringing stone from Ancaster, the builders brought most of it from Barnack in Northamptonshire, along the rivers and fen drains. No reason for these grand – and for the population, much oversized – churches has ever been found, other than the prosperity of Boston, and the pride of the great monasteries at Croyland and Spalding, whose fervour and spirituality inspired the building of these fine churches to the glory of God.

First, there are the spires, pointing to Heaven, the spire of Swineshead rising from a low octagon surmounting a magnificent Perpendicular tower; the octagonal spire of Fleet, of noble Decorated proportions; the remarkable

Early English lead spire of Long Sutton, 'the highest, oldest, and most perfect lead spire in England', wrote Doctor J. Charles Cox; the tapering broach spire of Holbeach, set back behind a battlemented parapet; the Perpendicular spire of Moulton, of great height and elegance; the leaning spire of Surfleet; the finely proportioned Perpendicular spire of Quadring; the grand spire of Donington crowning a spacious vaulted south-west porch; last, but by no means least, Frampton, where a solid, square Transitional tower is crowned with a splendid Early English broach spire.

Who can forget the Norman nave at Long Sutton, with triforium and Perpendicular clerestory; the monastic Norman nave at Freiston; the truncated Norman nave at Bicker or the long Transitional nave at Whaplode? Who can forget the elegant lofty nave at Holbeach, built just when Decorated was turning into Perpendicular, or the Early English church at Weston St Mary, or the Early English clustered columns of the nave at Wyberton, with its unexpected small Georgian apsidal chancel? What of the towers of Holland? The rare Early English tower at Whaplode, the elegant Perpendicular tower at Pinchbeck, the several Perpendicular towers at Freiston and Benington, at Leverton, and at Old Leake with its sumptuously adorned Decorated nave and chancel? Two brick Perpendicular towers with stone spires, at Lutton and Tydd St Mary, must be mentioned, too. Nor can we forget the important fourteenth-century glass at Wrangle, with its rich deep colours. No church in the county can boast so much.

In addition to all these, there are four churches which deserve a few extra lines to themselves. The first is Gosberton. Alec Clifton-Taylor wrote an important book entitled *English Parish Churches as Works of Art* (Batsford, 1974). Gosberton certainly qualifies for such a description. It is cruciform, with central tower and crocketed spire, all built at the time when Decorated was turning into Perpendicular. Elegant flying buttresses support the spire, decorative embattled parapets crown the clerestory, the traceried windows around the church are Decorated or Perpendicular, the transepts are lofty, the interior spacious and many-vistaed. It is, especially when viewed from the south side, a beautiful composition – a work of art.

Algarkirk is another such, cruciform again, with central tower and lower lead spire, all a masterpiece of Early English, Decorated or Perpendicular, happily merging with one another. It is like a miniature cathedral in plan and in its spacious park-like setting, with wonderful aisled transepts adorned with sumptuous traceried Decorated windows. It was handsomely restored *circa* 1850 by the scholarly hands of R. C. and R. H. Carpenter (architects of Lancing College), and it is thanks to them that we have the mellow, colourful interior with vistas everywhere, the splendidly furnished chancel and the skilfully placed organ; the chancel and south transept windows are by Hardman, the rest by Clayton and Bell. The whole church proclaims the Tractarian ideals of the restorers. There are many monuments to the Beridge family, who were squarsons here from the seventeenth to the nineteenth century. Prebendary Basil Beridge, who built the churches at Amber Hill and Fosdyke out of his own pocket, was Rector here for nearly sixty years, and its generous benefactor, also.

It is an altogether different story at Kirton-in-Holland – and an astonishing one. This handsome church presides splendidly over the main street, with its long line of Perpendicular clerestory windows, its Decorated traceried windows below, Perpendicular clerestory and magnificent Perpendicular tower at the west end, and Perpendicular chancel. However, there exists a drawing of Kirton Church, *circa* 1829, drawn by Stephen Lewen, engraved by Madeley and published by P. Morton of Boston in 1843, showing something altogether different: a cruciform church, with a double aisled south transept, forming a magnificent frontis-piece to the street, with a grand central tower above and

Perpendicular chancel to the east. How can this picture be reconciled with what we see today? The fact is that in 1804 the architect, William Hayward of Lincoln, demolished the central tower and the transepts, rebuilt the tower at the west end, and rebuilt the chancel on the site of the crossing. It is an incredible, even shocking story. It is the more amazing that everything fits together as it does; it is a brilliant piece of pastiche. But would that we could see this magnificent church as it was. Even so, it is an exceptionally fine and most interesting church; with its lofty, six-bay Early English nave, the interior, beautifully furnished by Temple Moore and others, is exceptionally numinous. It is indeed a solemn, devotional church.

In the Fens, the churches sail past like ships at sea. It is a thrill just to watch Gedney sail into view. It is almost transparent with its lofty clerestory of twelve lights, its rows of traceried windows below. The tower is very lofty and built in three stages – Early English, Decorated and Perpendicular – and the base of a spire was begun; but the foundations, or funds, or spirits failed them. Even with only the little lead spire, this tower is extremely impressive. A grand two-storeyed porch leads into the nave (the door itself is fourteenth-century, too) to the delights of some fourteenth-century glass, seventeenth-century pulpit, and seventeenth-century Welby monuments. It is a church with a great presence.

## The Churches of Kesteven

There are aboundingly good churches in Kesteven, too. 'From almost any church tower near Sleaford', says *Murray's Handbook*, 'fifteen or twenty spires can be counted'. One soon loses count: looking east we can count Ewerby, Asgarby, Heckington, Helpringham; and, round to the south, Scredington, Aswarby, Aunsby, Pickworth,

Sapperton, Wilsford, Welby, Kelby, Ancaster, Rauceby; round to the west and north, Leasingham, Ashby, Digby and Billinghay. Looking a little farther afield, along the Grantham-Lincoln road are Barkston, Caythorpe, Leadenham, Wellingore, Brant Broughton, Coleby, Branston; further afield again, Marston, and the leaning spire of Dry Doddington. Nearer Grantham are Gonerby and Barrowby, Harlaxton; further south again, Bassing-thorpe and Bitchfield; the list goes on interminably. There is that wonderful point on the A15, just south of the roundabout, where the road south crosses the Bridge End Road and the view opens out in all its magnificence, with the broach spire of Threckingham to the east, the tapering crocketed broach spire of Walcot to the west, the pinnacled tower of Folkingham ahead, Rippingale tower further on, the fens beyond that; not long after, Billingborough's magical spire comes in sight. It was here that the author, at the age of fifteen, on his first bicycle, began to absorb the splendour of the churches of Kesteven.

All Kesteven is resplendent with wonderful churches, for here is the glorious Ancaster stone, and almost every village can boast a great church, if not on the scale of the fen churches, at least on a noble scale for a village. There are not only spires, but grand towers also: Folkingham, already mentioned, or Fulbeck, or Boothby Pagnell, or Great Ponton; pride of place must go to Hough-on-the-Hill, a grand Saxon tower, with a Perpendicular pinnacled top and its very rare extruding staircase turret.

There are too many churches in Kesteven to describe in any detail; but a few must be mentioned. Heckington is one of the greatest and grandest Decorated churches anywhere, owing its magnificence to the wealthy Bardney Abbey. Walk round the exterior and absorb its many details: the great curvilinear windows, the crocketed pinnacles, the traceried parapets, the south porch with its carvings, the tremendous tower and spire; then, finally, the chancel with its early window of seven lights, comparable with those at Carlisle and Selby. Then go inside, absorb the spaciousness, and then the amazing chancel with its Easter Sepulchre and Sedilia. These are the finest in England.

Not far away is Heydour, a tiny hamlet; the large church with its lofty spire is a happy marriage of Early English, Decorated and Perpendicular. There is important fourteenth-century glass and a wealth of monuments to the Newtons of Culverthorpe (nearby) in the north chapel. Two by Rysbrack, two by Scheemakers, they are to be discovered only by the most persistent seeker, hidden by the organ, approached through an old baize door.

Sedgebrook is entirely different: the glory of many Kesteven churches is Early English or Decorated; at Sedgebrook the glory is Perpendicular; there is one earlier arcade – the rest is all Perpendicular. It is built of silvery Ancaster stone and golden ironstone, and the sunlight pours into a spacious, glistening, white interior, picking out ancient screens, chancel stalls, pulpit and carved, stone canopied niches and sedilia in the lofty chancel. The great rebuilding was due to Sir John Markham, 'the upright judge' in 1468ff.

Swaton is one of the lesser-known marvels of Lincolnshire, a grand cruciform church not far from the fens. It is always a thrill to push open the north door and to stand confronted by the spacious nave, its aisles almost as lofty as the nave itself, by the enormous traceried windows, and the font adorned with diapering and bellflower ornament. All this is Decorated: to turn east and look through the lower, narrower crossing arches into the chancel with its lancet windows is to move into the earlier world of Early English. It is a pleasure just to walk round this beautiful church, with the daylight pouring in on old pew ends and old stone floors.

Pickworth is another wonderful church – in the unfrequented Stone Belt – almost entirely Decorated, with a broach spire and an 'unrestored' interior of old pews, medieval rood screen of the most delicate workmanship, seventeenth-century two-decker pulpit, eighteenth-century altar rails and important fourteenth-century wall paintings, now being restored by Elizabeth Hirst. The Doom is over the chancel arch; figures are sizzling in a cauldron on the south wall, but the friendly figure of St Christopher is opposite, and nearby the ascending Christ.

Norton Disney is a romantic, unsophisticated church lost in the willows of the River Witham, south-west of Lincoln, with wonderful tombs and brasses (one a palimpsest) of the Disneys. A perfect village church of many dates.

Nocton is that rare thing in Lincolnshire, a Victorian village church. This magnificent church by Sir George Gilbert Scott (1862) was built for the Countess of Ripon in memory of her husband, who (as Viscount Goderich) had been Prime Minister in 1827–8. Glowing with marble and alabaster, the interior is sumptuous and stately – a remarkable contrast to most of our churches.

But there is an echo of this at Belton, where the little church (Norman and later) is crammed with a most remarkable collection of tombs and monuments to the Brownlows, from the seventeenth century to the present day; works by the foremost sculptors of every generation. 'Belton Church was built to the glory of the Brownlows, and in memory of God,' remarked Harry Cust, politician and wit, and great grandson of the first Lord Brownlow.

The length of this Kesteven collection is almost overwhelming, but two must be added: Brant Broughton and Stragglethorpe, so near geographically, so different in every other way. Brant Broughton is one of the most distinguished of all Lincolnshire churches. In 1873, Canon F. H. Sutton – scholar, antiquary, collector, artist, and friend of G. F. Bodley – was appointed to this family living. Brant Broughton was already in its own right a major church. With a spire one hundred and ninety feet high, the church itself is mostly fourteenth-century, with two lavish porches and much wonderful medieval decoration, but in 1872 there was only a poor mean chancel, built in 1812. The remarkable partnership of Sutton and Bodley meant that a new chancel was built on the medieval foundations, grafted on to the medieval nave: wonderful furnishings were designed for the church, and in his own workshop at the rectory Canon Sutton made glass of very high quality for almost every window in the church. It is a glorious interior, like a medieval dream.

Stragglethorpe Church stands in a farmyard, an enchanting little medieval church; Norman and later, it is very little altered over the centuries. Moreover, it preserves undisturbed its Georgian interior with bleached box pews, two-decker pulpit, plastered ceiling, and splendid monument (by Green of Camberwell, 1697) to Sir Richard Earle, third and last Baronet. There is a long, touching, verse inscription:

Stay, Reader and observe Death's Partial Doom.

Alas, that we cannot.


## The Churches of Lindsey

The churches of Lindsey are quite different from the churches of Kesteven and Holland: smaller for the most part, and many of them older, sometimes displaying important pre-Conquest work and Anglo-Saxon towers. Lindsey in area is roughly half the county – the equivalent of Kesteven and Holland together.

Stow comes to mind: rising above the red roofs of its small village stands this incredible fortress-like church. There is nothing in all England to compare with the tremendous tenth-century Saxon crossing, later strengthened by additional arches to carry the fourteenth-century tower. Nave and transepts are Early Norman, the chancel a little later. Here, in 1868, J. L. Pearson skilfully rebuilt the vaulting, a remarkable feat. Not far away, to the east, but lost in the middle of a farm, is Cotes-by-Stow, mentioned in Chapter V, a precious, tiny church, Norman and later, filled with wonderful woodwork, old seats, medieval pulpit and screen, complete with rood loft.

Close to the Trent stands Marton, a thrilling church with grand Saxon tower and a splendid display of 'herringbone' masonry – to be found in the walls of the church, too. It is a most important church.

Laughton is another special church. Here Bodley, in collaboration with the Hon. Mrs Meynell-Ingram, gloriously re-edified the church (1896) in memory of her husband, to whose memory she had also built the church at Hoar Cross (Staffordshire). Here, Bodley raised the nave and built the lofty chancel; glorious Bodley furnishings include the wonderful reredos and ornaments for the altar.

Bottesford, nearby, is also a thrilling church, pure Early English, with elegant arcades and a delightful rhythm of long lancets and circular windows. A church which deserves to be better known.

Barton-on-Humber surveys the Humber and looks across to Yorkshire. Its two churches are of great importance and interest. St Peter's must be the oldest church in Lincolnshire, and architecturally of prime importance, with its remarkable Saxon tower and little Saxon nave (to the west). It is now in the hands of the Department of the Environment, which has carried out important excavations. St Mary's is the medieval 'Chapel of Ease'. Some Chapel of Ease! Excellent Early English nave and chancel – all built on a generous scale. Here, in the north of the county, are a number of impressive Anglo-Saxon or early Norman towers; at Broughton is another noble tower with an extruding stair turret, similar to Hough-on-the-Hill (in Kesteven); the only two others in England are at Brixworth and Brigstock in Northamptonshire. Simpler Anglo-Saxon towers are at Scartho, Old Clee, and Rothwell. This is an altogether delightful church, with Norman nave and chancel restored and furnished by J. D. Sedding in 1892. Two churches are worth a special visit for their monuments: Hainton and Snarford, but details of these will be found in Chapter III.

There is an enchanting set of small eighteenth-century churches in Lindsey, mostly connected with a squire's house nearby. At Gautby, the great house of the Vyners was pulled down more than a century ago (see pp. 94), but the atmosphere of a vanished house remains: garden walls, forgotten gardens, a stable building. The house was *circa* 1750, so is the little brick church, delightful with its modest tower and short lead spire. The interior is a delight, too, simple and honest, but with a grand entrance to the chancel framed by Ionic pilasters. Here, on either side of the altar, are two splendid late seventeenth-century Vyners, leaning on their elbows, so placed that they appear to be peering behind the altar curtains. They were removed from the London City church of St Mary Woolnoth and provide a touch of pomp and circumstance. Langton, a little earlier in date, is larger; and perfect with its wonderful interior, almost like a college chapel, with its three-decker pulpit, curving Communion rails, and reredos with fluted Corinthian pilasters; the woodwork is all of superb quality. It is very much the squire's church, and it is easy to imagine Doctor Johnson worshipping here with his friend Bennet Langton.

Well is a little later, and stands in James Bateman's beautiful landscape park. For a fuller account of this see p. 16.

Baumber is a baffling church: intriguing and massive, its eighteenth-century red brick exterior is found to enclose a medieval stone church within. But dividing the nave from the Georgian chancel is a screen of three ogee Gothick arches, playfully adorned with foliage, and so reminiscent of Shobdon in Herefordshire that it is tempting to ascribe Baumber to the same (unknown) hand: the pulpit canopies appear very similar, too.

Two others must be mentioned: Saxby St Helen, small but grand, 'with a touch of St George's Hanover Square', as the author, Sheila Sutcliffe, remarked: and Hannah, simple and unsophisticated among windswept sycamores near the coast.

At Langworth is another fascinating church, re-erected here thirty years ago: it is the former chapel at Walmsgate Hall, almost certainly by Henry Wilson. The Art Nouveau decoration is exquisite: it is a little building of the greatest charm.

In the Marsh, close to the sea is a special group of large medieval churches, quite different from the fen churches, but an equal pleasure. Croft is a most rewarding marshland church with fifteenth-century screens, a medieval brass lectern rescued from a moat, seventeenth-century monuments, old pews and pulpit, and an important brass. Burgh-le-Marsh has a tall Perpendicular tower, as already mentioned, and a devout interior, rich in sixteenth- and seventeenth-century woodwork. At Addlethorpe the sunlight pours through large clear glass windows on to ancient screen and pews – an interior of special charm. Theddlethorpe is the 'cathedral of the Marsh'. Outside the texture is all greenstone and old brick; inside there is an array of unusual ancient screens, a medieval stone reredos, a fifteenth-century brass and two good eighteenth-century monuments. Saltfleetby All Saints is endearing with its gently leaning tower and long low nave, with weighty, humpy, lead roof almost slipping off its crown.

Further inland are two other notable churches: the first is Tattershall, greatest and grandest Perpendicular church in Lincolnshire, standing beside the famous castle. It was founded as a collegiate church by Ralph, Lord Cromwell in the middle of the fifteenth century, though not a trace of the collegiate buildings survives. It is a magnificent building, and sunlight pours through its enormous clear glass windows on to an interior of slightly forlorn beauty. A stone screen, surmounted by an organ, divides nave from chancel: in the north transept are some of the finest brasses in the county.

Not far away, and hard to find in its setting of bumpy fields, close to the gaunt fragment of the south transept of the great abbey, stands Kirkstead Chapel, the *capella ante portas* of the great Cistercian house. It is a tiny, exquisite, vaulted Early English church with narrow lancets, delicately carved capitals and dwarf shafts. This most precious little church might serve as a fitting climax to our collection of country churches.

# XVI
# Vanished Houses of Lincolnshire

Writing in the Introduction to the *Shell Guide to Lincoln-shire* (Faber and Faber 1965), the authors remarked, 'There is a "goneness" about Lincolnshire that is difficult to capture in words.' This has already been remarked upon here, in the survey of lost Lincolnshire railways (Chapter XII). It is perhaps even more telling in the case of the country houses. Hugh Montgomery-Massingberd has written: 'In Lincolnshire there were over two hundred squires flourishing in their family seats in the 1880s; today there are barely four dozen.' This means a wastage rate of over seventy-five per cent, though in fact the national average is as high as eighty-five per cent. This is grim. Looking across the county, the sight of broken down walls, broken down gatepiers and gates, cedar trees on a hillside presiding over an empty site – and cedars are always a sign of civilisation – are symbols of the vanishing squirearchy.

In Lindsey, Panton is a case in point. In the eighteenth century, the Turnors of Stoke Rochford (*q.v.*) acquired Panton Hall near Wragby, and much property all around. Panton Hall was begun for Joseph Gace by William Talman in 1714, and (after Talman's death) completed by Nicholas Hawksmoor. Later in the century, the wings were added by John Carr of York. It was a splendid house, of impressive architectural lineage, but all now is laid low. The Turnors sold all their property in and around Panton, and Wragby, in the early twentieth century. There were two or three owners thereafter, and then this most interesting and impressive house was destroyed. The house stood on its low hill, a magnificent sight: all that remains is the great stable quadrangle . . . empty . . . no horses.

For atmosphere a visit should be paid to Gautby nearby. Here the house was demolished over one hundred years ago (1872), but the old brick walls surrounding the garden still stand, as does one stable building. The house was perhaps by Matthew Brettingham; and on an island in the lake, now largely silted up, stood that grand equestrian statue of Charles II, now gracing the grounds at Newby Hall, near Ripon. Sir Robert Vyner was goldsmith to Charles II, and made the new regalia for his Coronation. The Vyner family inherited the grander property at Newby: Gautby was left to moulder, and then demolished. There are moving memorials to the family in the little eighteenth-century church.

Not very far away, near Market Rasen, stood the most romantic ruins of Bayons Manor, built between 1836 and 1840 by Tennyson's uncle, Charles Tennyson-d'Eyncourt, Member of Parliament for Lambeth. The story of the house and the family who built it will be familiar. The poet's grandfather decided to pass over his elder son, George, in favour of his younger brother, Charles, who was thought the more likely to promote the glory of the Tennyson family. George was forced by his father to take Holy Orders, a calling to which he felt himself unsuited, and throughout his life found uncongenial. Yet it was his son who made the name Tennyson immortal.

Charles built this remarkable, bogus, medieval fortified manor. What began as a modest Regency house was encrusted in an impressive Gothic covering, and to this were added great hall, library, and other large reception rooms, and a tower. An immense castellated wall was built to surround this, a moat and barbican, gatehouse and draw-bridge, and all was so ingeniously devised that it was necessary to make a complete circuit of the defences to reach the front door. There was a huge ruined keep on the hill behind. It was magnificent. But a century later, the family had left, and thirty years ago what had become already a beautiful ruin was blown up. A tragedy.

An avenue leading to nothing, or an empty park, accompanied by a church with an array of family monuments: these are things which provide clues to the site of a vanished house. The long, long avenue at Spilsby leads to Eresby, once the great seat of the Willoughbys and Berties; it was burnt in 1769 and never rebuilt. Grimsthorpe (*q.v.*) had already taken its place. There does not even seem to be a picture surviving of Eresby, only the solitary grand gatepier, capped by its grandiloquent urn. Another solitary gatepier stands at Stainfield, close to the little Queen Anne church, to mark the site of Stainfield Hall, seat of the Tyrwhitts of Stainfield, a many-gabled Elizabethan house. But pictures do exist of the house, which burned down in 1855: the white brick early nineteenth-century farmhouse occupies its site, and the family are called to mind by the panels of faded embroidery in the church, worked by Tyrwhitt ladies in the early eighteenth century. Go to Bigby to see the magnificent Elizabethan tombs of the Tyrwhitts of Kettleby – the senior line – but there is nothing left of Kettleby, just the inevitable farmhouse occupying the site. Perhaps the most poignant of all is Snarford, its little church in the middle of nowhere. The door of this modest building opens to reveal the theatrical display of grand Elizabethan or Jacobean tombs and monuments to the St Paul family (see p. 14). House, garden, park, the family themselves, their wealth, even their name have all vanished: only the monuments are still here to recall their memory.

Another poignant broken relic is the derelict shell of Glentworth Hall, designed by James Paine in 1753 for the third Earl of Scarbrough. The Scarbroughs had acquired by marriage all the property in Lincolnshire and elsewhere of the Saundersons, Viscounts Castleton, who had themselves acquired all the property of the Wrays, the descendants of the Lord Chief Justice, Sir Christopher Wray, whose splendid tomb is in the church. Behind Paine's long façade is a small fragment – an archway and two or three mullioned windows – of Sir Christopher's Elizabethan house; a drawing of this survives in the Bodleian. Paine's house was never completed; only the handsome façade facing east up the hill was built, together with the stables. The Earl, apparently, changed his mind and employed Paine instead to build Sandbeck Hall (in the West Riding), which became the Scarbroughs' principal seat, as indeed it is today. The sad wreck of Glentworth appears almost a phantom from the hillside.

So much for the losses in Lindsey; it is the same in Kesteven. We can start with Blankney, famous for its Hunt. 'Blankney', wrote Sir Osbert Sitwell in *The Scarlet Tree*, 'stood a dead weight in the snow. For us it loomed large at the end of each year, and the roads of every passing month led nearer to it, an immense stone building of regular appearance, echoing in rhythm the empty syllables of its name.' Blankney was his grandparents' home. Occupied by the Royal Air Force in the Second World War, it was burnt out in 1945. So passed a great sporting seat of Lincolnshire. But the fire revealed that Sir Osbert's 'immense stone building of regular appearance' was not in fact the solid eighteenth-century mansion that it appeared. Behind the grand Palladian façade were the tall Elizabethan gables of the house built by Sir Anthony Thorold. It passed to his daughter who married the first Lord Widdrington, Royalist Commander in the Civil War. The Widdringtons, recusant and Jacobite, lost all in the '15 Rebellion. The Chaplins took over, till the great Henry Chaplin's extravagance on the turf brought all to an end. Lord Londesborough, the chief mortgagee, acquired Blankney and the Londesboroughs provided the final brilliant chapter in Blankney's history.

Haverholme Priory was pulled down in 1927. It was in

origin a Gilbertine priory, founded in 1139 and one of the most important Gilbertine houses, with fifty monks and one hundred nuns. Thomas à Becket, Archbishop of Canterbury took refuge there in 1164. After the Dissolution, part of the monastic house was converted into a secular house, later prettily gothicised by the Gordon baronets, and then largely rebuilt in Victorian Tudor by H. E. Kendall for the Earl of Winchilsea. Most of this was demolished in 1927; one tower survives, together with garden walls and gates. The Slea Navigation passes through the grounds.

Grantham has always been celebrated for the great country houses that surround the town: Belvoir, Harlaxton, Stoke Rochford, Denton, Easton, Syston, Belton. Three of these, each the seat of a baronet, have been pulled down, but in every case the family has continued to live there, albeit in a smaller house. The Welbys at Denton had replaced the old house with a grand neo-Tudor mansion designed by Sir A. W. Blomfield (1883). This was pulled down in 1939; after the war, Marshall Sisson and Peter Foster built the delightful new house for Sir Oliver Welby, sixth Baronet, on to the small nucleus of the original seventeenth-century house which survived in the stable court.

The Cholmeleys have been established at Easton since the late sixteenth century, an offshoot of the great Cheshire Cholmondeley family. There have been earlier houses, but in emulation of Stoke Rochford and Harlaxton, a large new Victorian Tudor house was built. It was neither greatly admired, nor long lived. The family took to the Dower House in the park, and the stable yard of the big house survives with its gatehouse, together with the romantic terraced gardens on either side of the river – now much overgrown.

The great house on the hill at Syston was built in 1766 onwards by Sir John Thorold, ninth Baronet; the park had already been planted and landscaped by the fourth Baronet in the early eighteenth century. It was a Palladian composition of three storeys, designed by the local architect John Langwith, with grand curving walls to connect it to the kitchen and stable blocks. In the next century, enormous additions were made for the tenth Baronet, the great book collector, for whom Vulliamy built the celebrated library and other additions. The house became a palace. The collection of books was no mere country house library; there were many very valuable volumes. The Mazarin Bible was sold in 1884, for £3,200, at that time the highest price for a single volume ever recorded. It went to America. When sold again recently, it fetched £1,000,000. The old hall at Syston, with its Jacobean porch and enormous courtyard, became the seat of the baronet, and the original family home at Marston, nearby, first acquired by marriage in the fourteenth century, is still in the possession of the family and is the home of the author of this book. It is of interest to find agreeable eighteenth-century rooms fitted into what was the sixteenth-century great hall.

At Aswarby the great house of the Whichcotes, Baronets, has been pulled down. In origin a Tudor house, the home of the Carres of Sleaford, it was acquired by Sir Christopher Whichcote, third Baronet, in the early eighteenth century it was much rebuilt by Kendall in the early nineteenth century. This has been pulled down, and the stables have been converted into a spacious house for the family. The first Baronet, Sir Jeremy, so created in 1660, was Solicitor General to the Prince Elector; his brother Benjamin was the eminent Cambridge Platonist, and Provost of King's.

On the Great North Road between Stamford and Grantham, there is, a few miles south of Colsterworth, a signpost pointing east to Lobthorpe. What is Lobthorpe, where is Lobthorpe? It is a pretty, well-wooded lane, which seems to lead inconsequently towards the village of Swayfield. But before we reach Swayfield there is a clearing on the south side, and a large stone farmhouse, a cottage or two. This is Lobthorpe. Here, till the late eighteenth century, stood the seat of the Sherards, Baronets. The farm has a pleasant prospect south across open country. But to find traces of the Sherards it is necessary to go to North Witham, a short distance on the west side of the Great North Road. Here in the church will be found a great gathering of monuments to the Sherards, occupying the entire chancel, works by Joshua Marshall, several by Edward Stanton and Christopher Horsnaile, and Edward Sharpe of Stamford; a handsome and eloquent collection.

Here lies the body of Sir John Sherard of
Lobthorpe in the County of Lincoln, Bart.

1724


Near this monument lies interred the body of Sir
Richard Sherard of Lobthorpe in this County, Bart.

1730


Among those of his Ancestors lie the remains of
Sir Brownlow Sherard of Lobthorpe in this County, Bart.

1736

and so on.

Lobthorpe Hall has vanished. All other traces of the family have vanished, but these grand works in marble remain, and explain that signpost on the Great North Road.

# XVII

## Lincolnshire Houses
## and their Families: Lindsey

On 4 November 1991 the night sky in the Lincolnshire
Wolds was illuminated for miles around by the tremendous
flames which very nearly destroyed Harrington Hall, near
Spilsby. The fire was started by a builder's blow-lamp, used
for removing old paint, during the redecoration of the house
for its new owners, Mr and Mrs David Price. Mr and Mrs
Price were actually searching for a country house in
Pembrokeshire. But somehow their steps were led inexplic-
ably to Lincolnshire (with which they had slight connections), and to Harrington in particular, with which they
immediately fell in love.

In the evening on 4 November, alerted by telephone, they
sped north from London, arriving at 11.30 p.m. to find the
outer walls still standing, but much of the interior a burnt
out shell. Now, four years later, the house has been
restored, and they are in residence; phoenix-like,
Harrington has risen from the ashes, more beautiful than
ever, thanks to their architect, Mr Guy St John Taylor of
Newark, and their builders, Messrs Taskers of Digby – and
thanks, above all, to Mr and Mrs Price themselves, whose
faith in the future of Harrington is a tonic to all lovers of
Lincolnshire houses. After the gloom of Chapter XVI, the
story of Harrington brings new hope for the future.

Harrington, as need hardly be said, is an enchanting
house of mellow red brick, with its long row of twelve sash
windows, interrupted in the centre by what is clearly a tall
Elizabethan porch tower. The house is in origin Elizabethan, built by the Copledyke family whose splendid

tombs are in the church. The Copledykes faded out (their last monument is of Thomas Copledyke, 1658) and Vincent Amcotts bought it, and remodelled the house. The date on the weather vane is 1678; the date on the sundial, 1681; these give a clue to the date of the remodelling, but much remains of the Elizabethan house, the stone plinth on which it stands, and (as has been said) the tall porch tower, which is a quite captivating feature of the front. On either side are two rows of six sash windows, which are perhaps an eighteenth-century replacement of seventeenth-century windows. Inside the porch, the fire has revealed the Tudor arched screens entrance; the screens passage now opens into the hall by means of a wide elliptical arch, which must take the place of the screens. Handsome eighteenth-century panelled rooms have been restored with great skill and sympathy.

The house is not all; it is surrounded by a garden of rare and special interest. Mellow brick walls and gatepiers capped with urns enclose it, steps lead up to seventeenth-century terrace walks, from which the gardens may be surveyed. Very few such terraced gardens survive in England. The garden inspired Tennyson when he wrote 'Come into the garden, Maud'.

Only a few miles from Harrington stands another specially captivating house: Gunby, seat of the Massingberds. Here stands a William and Mary house in plum-coloured brick, with stone dressings, three storeys high like a big, lovable doll's house. It was built by Sir William Massingberd, the second Baronet in 1700 (the date over the front door), and the story of its rescue in 1944 from a threatened runway from a nearby wartime airfield has already been told in Chapter II. It is due to that distinguished soldier, Field-Marshal Sir Archibald Montgomery-Massingberd, and his wife that this enchanting house still stands. The baronetcy died out, and Gunby passed sideways for several generations through different allied families (in particular the Langtons of nearby Langton). It seems always to have been specially loved and cherished by the family, which gives it its very special charm and family atmosphere. Inside, there are very pretty panelled rooms, a distinguished staircase, and one grand mid-Victorian drawing-room, so skilfully added by an unknown architect that it seems in no way an innovation. Here hang Sir Joshua's superb portraits of Bennet Langton and his wife, the Dowager Countess of Rothes. There are wonderful gardens, in particular two immense walled gardens, a romantic long canal and intimate smaller gardens, one presided over by a little domed garden seat, and great cedars to shade each spreading lawn.

But a few miles to the north-west is Langton, home of the Langtons, one of the two or three very oldest Lincolnshire families; they have been here since the twelfth century, taking their name from the place where they have always lived. Alas, there is no great house surviving; the charming Elizabethan house, home of Bennet Langton (see Gunby) Doctor Johnson's friend, was burnt; an eighteenth-century successor was pulled down – as was a Victorian house (1866) by James Fowler. Now, a delightful round *cottage orné*, with thatched roof, leads up a short lime avenue to the charming white-painted Langton Cottage (cottage in eighteenth-century terms), the present home of the family. The eighteenth-century church, as has been said elsewhere, is a particularly complete and perfect early eighteenth-century building. It is a pleasure to think of Doctor Johnson and Bennet Langton attending divine service there.

Only a few miles to the north is South Ormsby, seat of the Massingberd-Mundys, and it is of special interest as the work of James Paine (1752). The Massingberd-Mundys of South Ormsby descend from Sir Drayner Massingberd, who was second son of Thomas Massingberd of Gunby; the male line failing in the early nineteenth century, their heir married a Mundy of Markeaton, Derbyshire. South

Ormsby is a red brick Georgian house, standing in a beautiful well wooded park, in a specially lovely valley of the Wolds. As originally built, the house was crowned by a magnificent pediment which stretched across the whole width of the east front – a typical James Paine feature. This was unfortunately removed fifty years later when Peter Atkinson added wings behind. The house, with front door in the canted bay of the east front, though it lacks the dramatic feature of Paine's great pediment, is still delightful. Inside, Paine's remarkable mahogany staircase is a work of great distinction.

Nearer Horncastle, but only a few miles away, is Scrivelsby, seat of the Champion. As is well known, the Lord of the Manor has the right, granted by the Conqueror, of acting as King's or Queen's Champion, and challenging all comers to the right of the Sovereign to the throne. Originally, the Champion rode into the Coronation banquet in Westminster Hall and threw down his challenge; after rowdy scenes at George IV's Coronation, the banquet was discontinued; the Champion now carries one of the standards at the Coronation itself. The Dymoke family acquired the Championship rights by marriage with the Marmions in the fourteenth century, and has carried out its romantic duty, at every Coronation since. The old house (shown in the Buck print of 1727) was destroyed by fire, and replaced by an unexciting early nineteenth-century house. This, the present Champion (Colonel John Dymoke) pulled down after the Second World War, and converted the Tudor gatehouse into a delightful house for his family. The park, with specially beautiful beech trees, and deer, provides a wonderful setting for the moated garden and gatehouse, approached by the ancient Lion Gate, most romantic of all park entrances.

But a few miles away, at Ulceby Cross, the road east leads to Alford; along this road there are two small signposts pointing to Well; either narrow lane will lead us to Well

Vale. There is already some account of this small paradise in Chapter IV and the link with Shobdon in Herefordshire has been stressed. James Bateman, brother of the first Lord Bateman of Shobdon, bought Well *circa* 1720, and proceeded to build (or rebuild) the house. The west front, of which the widely spaced centre is crowned with a low pediment, is serenely beautiful and restrained; devoid of decoration, its subtle proportions and warm plum-coloured brick speak for themselves. It is perhaps the remodelling of an older house: there are clues both outside and inside which suggest that this may be so. There is no clue as to who the architect may have been, nor as to who landscaped the park and built the church in 1733, so happily aligned on the front door of the house. The place passed by marriage to the Dashwood family; later to the Rawnsleys.

Across the park to the south is the little hamlet of Claxby. James Bateman bought the place in 1729, and after his wife's death built the small but distinguished house here, with handsome interiors and splendid plasterwork, a miniature grand house. Over the stairs in plaster are the arms of James Bateman and his wife, Ann Chaplin. Two hundred years later, after the death of Major Walter Rawnsley, his widow (*née* Chaplin) came to live here and created the beautiful garden. Her son and daughter-in-law, Major and Mrs J. R. C. Rawnsley, added to the gardens at Well, with lawns sloping from the house to the lakes.

It is sad to have to add that Well has been empty for several years and is now occupied by a school – good tenants no doubt, but much of the garden has gone. Even so, Well Vale remains the most beautiful setting for any house, 'here at the quiet limit of the Wolds'.

To the north-west is Hainton, where the Heneages have lived since the fourteenth century, and still live. The road from Louth to Wragby skirts the park, landscaped by Capability Brown in 1763; the house is visible through the trees. It is an ancient house, but has been much altered over the centuries. What must have been the Tudor Great Hall still occupies an important part of the south front, and next to it is an octagonal turret, crowned by an ogee-shaped cupola, clearly of Elizabethan date. The west front became the entrance front in the eighteenth century and the architect, Peter Atkinson, added a second floor and covered the whole house in grey stucco, which gave the great mansion a gloomy appearance. The east wing (which balanced this) was pulled down in the 1950s; the present squire has ingeniously removed the cement, and in place of the east wing has erected an octagonal kitchen wing crowned with a small ogee-shaped dome, to echo its smaller octagonal counterpart – an original device to complete the south front. Inside, there is a handsome two-storeyed hall, dating from the mid-eighteenth century – the Georgianised Tudor Great Hall – and other early eighteenth-century rooms, in addition to Atkinson's grand late-Georgian rooms in the west wing. In its splendid setting of well wooded countryside, Hainton is a very precious Lincolnshire landmark; the oldest family mansion to be continuously occupied by its historic family for over six hundred years.

Reference has already been made in Chapter XV to the church, with its remarkable monuments dating from 1435 to the present day; one of the finest family collections in England. It was Capability Brown who suggested adding the spire to the tower, to provide an eye catcher across the park; so it does today, as we travel from Louth to Wragby, gazing across the park.

To the north lies Brocklesby, seat of the Earls of Yarborough. Brocklesby was constructed on a far grander scale than anything we have so far considered. Approaching from Kirmington, we reach the great memorial arch across the road 'To Charles Anderson Worsley second Earl of Yarborough by his Tenants and Friends 1864'. The Earl died in 1862. This sets the scale for everything. There are lodges, temples, monuments on every convenient site; the park, as already mentioned, was landscaped by Capability Brown in 1770ff. Close to the site of Newsham Abbey, the first Premonstratensian house in Britain (1143), of which nothing remains, stands the Newsham Bridge, somewhat monastic in its almost medieval details. Just outside the park is the railway station (1848), a handsome building in the Jacobean style (by Weightman and Hadfield) with a glorious waiting room for the Earl and his family. The second Earl was Chairman of the Manchester, Sheffield and Lincolnshire Railway (later Great Central).

The founder of the Yarborough dynasty was Sir William Pelham, younger son of Sir William Pelham of Laughton, Sussex; from the elder son descended the Dukes of Newcastle and the Earls of Chichester. Sir William of Brocklesby was a distinguished military commander and field-marshal in the reign of Elizabeth I. Over the centuries his descendants have steadily built up the great estate and benevolently dominated the district. It is the great feudal capital of this remote part of Lincolnshire. The present house is a grand, early-Georgian building of brick with stone dressings and was built *circa* 1730, facing east. Enormous additions were made during the next century or so, when the long south front was built, in different stages; it had a certain magnificence, but was not a happy composition. In 1898 a great fire broke out, destroying most of the interior. This was rebuilt by Sir Reginald Blomfield, but in 1962ff Claud Phillimore was commissioned to pull down almost all of these extensions and return the house to its original state. It is still a large house —and all the finer for the loss of the nineteenth-century additions.

Brocklesby is in every way a great demesne: stables and kennels are close to the house, walled gardens, lodges, the estate offices; the park, the lake and its bridge, the temples and monuments, even the church itself, all contribute to the charm and splendour of the setting. The church is Decorated in date; it houses the early and the recent family monuments, and a most elegant organ designed by James Wyatt (1778). A long wooded walk leads to the mausoleum, built in 1787ff by James Wyatt in memory of Sophia Aufrere, wife of the first Lord Yarborough. It is the architect's masterpiece and stands on a tumulus, surmounted by beautiful, melancholy cedars. It is domed and colonnaded, with twelve fluted Doric columns on a rusticated base, and with a frieze above, adorned with garlands and swags beneath the balustrade and the dome itself. Inside, glass in the dome by Francis Eginton provides the perfect light for the standing figure of Sophia by Joseph Nollekens.

A few miles to the west is Normanby, seat of the Sheffield family, although most of the house is now leased to the Borough of Scunthorpe as the Art Gallery and Museum. There have been earlier houses here at Normanby, and also in the Isle of Axholme, where the most ancient of the Sheffields lived: in the sixteenth century the family moved across the Trent to the higher ground of Normanby. Plans and designs exist of a grand and stately mansion for the family, apparently by Robert Smythson. It is not certain whether they were intended for Normanby or Butterwick, or Owston in the Isle of Axholme.

The first notable member of the family was Sir Robert, Speaker of the House of Commons, who was knighted after the Battle of Stoke (1467). His grandson became the first Baron Sheffield (1547) and his grandson, first Earl of Mulgrave, K.G. and President of the North. The first Duke of Buckingham, first Marquis of Normanby (1694), the statesman and friend of Pope and Dryden, was his grandson.

The present house here was built in 1825 by Sir Robert Smirke for Sir Robert Sheffield, fourth Baronet. It is a severe stone house, depending for its effect on proportion rather than on decoration, of which there is externally very little;

all depends on the architect's skilful interplay of cubic forms. Smirke's reception rooms and double staircase form a splendid setting for the Scunthorpe Art Gallery and Museum, though the family retain ownership and occupy the east wing (by Walter Brierley, 1905) in addition to another house on the estate.

North-east of Brigg is Elsham, home of the ancient and gifted family of Elwes. It would be tempting to derive the name of Elsham from Elwes-ham; indeed the author often indulges in this make-believe. In fact, the Elwes family, though an ancient Lincolnshire and Nottinghamshire family, with property at Saundby in Nottinghamshire and Roxby in Lincolnshire from the sixteenth century, had no seat in Lincolnshire for several centuries, their chief home being at Great Billing in Northamptonshire. However, in 1931 Colonel Geoffrey Elwes sold Billing and bought Elsham.

The property had descended from the Thompson family to the Corbetts at the end of the eighteenth century, and in the nineteenth to the Astleys, Baronets. Sir John Astley, third Baronet, and his son, Sir Francis Astley-Corbett, fourth Baronet, were in their time legendary sporting squires, but after the Great War they sold the estate to King's College, Cambridge; it was from the college that Colonel Elwes bought the estate in 1932.

The house then was a curiously misshapen building, with a tall eighteenth-century wing on the east side, and a lower, older centre and south side, much altered and patched. Colonel Elwes commissioned his brother Colonel Guy Elwes, the architect, to pull the house together. Guy Elwes was a genius with country houses, and he rebuilt the west wing to match the east, and built up the centre to provide a spacious hall, and, behind that, a most beautiful Roman Catholic Chapel; his great grandfather had embraced the Catholic faith in the aftermath of the Oxford Movement, when a number of distinguished Englishmen found stability and peace in the Roman Church.

Elsham is now a spacious and delightful house; Guy Elwes' library is specially handsome, and the views across park and gardens, up the long avenue or towards the lakes, are happily conceived. There is a charming eighteenth-century orangery, and the grand stable yard, with tall cupola, is a grand legacy from the era of sporting squires.

Colonel Geoffrey Elwes' nephew, Captain Jeremy Elwes, is now the owner, and since 1970 he has generously opened the park as a country and wildlife park and welcomes thousands of visitors to this captivating place, with its Barn Theatre and Granary Restaurant and all the other pleasures of farmyard and park. The house, however, is not open to the public.

Not far away, on the west side of Brigg, is Scawby, still the seat of the Nelthorpes. The park stretches to the gates of the town on the east side, but on the west the house stands protected by great walls of old brick close to its village; it is a romantic, rambling, early seventeenth-century house of mellow brick. The Nelthorpes were originally of Staplehurst in Kent and first came to Scawby by marriage in the sixteenth century, but were also lawyers in London. The baronetcy was conferred on John Nelthorpe of Gray's Inn in 1688. His monument is in Clerkenwell Church. He founded the flourishing Grammar School at Brigg in 1678. It is perhaps surprising that the family never rebuilt the house on a grand scale in the eighteenth century; but the survival of their old house is a pleasure for us, as are the monuments in Scawby church.

A few miles south of Brigg is Redbourne; a late eighteenth-century west front conceals an earlier house behind, long and straggling. Of great charm is the delightful little toy-fort Gothick gateway, surmounted by the royal lion, at the entrance to the drive. The property passed by marriage in the eighteenth century from the Carter family to the Dukes of St Albans, descendants of Charles II and Nell Gwynne. The church is specially remarkable with its

Gothick plasterwork and monuments, and a frightening window of the Day of Judgement by William Collins.

A few miles further south, almost at Caenby Corner, is that elegant classical screen, capped with urns, leading to Norton Place. Built for John Harrison, Member of Parliament for Lincoln, by John Carr, in 1776, it is one of Carr's most beautiful houses. It is perfect in size and setting; handsome rooms adorned with elegant plasterwork surround the oval central staircase hall, lit by a small dome, where the cantilevered stone staircase ascends, with the prettiest iron balustrade. John Harrison's daughter married Sir Montague Cholmeley, first Baronet of Easton, in 1801, whose family held it for a century or more; it has since passed to new owners who cherish it as it deserves.

Further south again is another Gothick gateway. This leads up a broad grand avenue of old trees to Fillingham Castle, a captivating Gothick, castellated house built in 1760 for Sir Cecil Wray. It is often ascribed to John Carr, and is certainly worthy of him with its round towers at the corners, crenellations and sash windows with Gothick glazing bars. On the west side, it stands on the edge of the cliff, with wide views across the lake below, known as Fillingham Broad. There is Gothick plaster vaulting in the hall, but most of the interiors are classical. The place passed sideways for several generations, then stood empty between the wars, while the owner lived in Brighton. It has now found new owners who love it and care for it.

Ermine Street will take us to one more distinguished house: Hackthorn, seat of the Cracroft family since the seventeenth century. The family originated at Cracroft Hall in Hogsthorpe parish, not far from the coast. There must have been a seventeenth-century house here, replaced by the present handsome neo-classical house at the very end of the eighteenth century. House and (early nineteenth-century) church make a lovely sight across this well wooded park. Inside, the house has fine rooms grouped round an oval

LINCOLNSHIRE HOUSES AND THEIR FAMILIES: LINDSEY

staircase hall, where the most elegant stairs rise, lit from above. Hackthorn is now the home of the present Lord Lieutenant of Lincolnshire, Mrs Robin Cracroft-Eley.

Only a few miles away, on the west side of Ermine Street is South Carlton, seat of the eleventh Lord Monson (pronounced Munson). The Monsons are an ancient Lincolnshire family, who have been in these parts since the fourteenth century, and at South Carlton since the early sixteenth century. South Carlton is tiny and charming. There is no village, merely a farmhouse or two, a cottage or two, the church, and the manor house. The church contains the great tomb by Nicholas Stone of Sir John Monson (erected 1625); there is a pond, protected by great weeping willows, facing the manor with the church next door. This was the old seat of the Monsons; in the eighteenth century they moved across to Burton, and James Paine built (on to an older nucleus) a new and handsome south front – a façade of nine stone bays. After the war, the tenth Lord Monson moved back to Carlton. It is, as it were, their *petit trianon*, an enchanting house, outwardly early-Georgian, but retaining fragments of the Tudor house which once stood here. It is the ideal house for today, and the present Lady Monson has formed a most beautiful garden around it. Much pleasure will be found here by garden-lovers when the auricula *Emma Monson* is in flower.

It was the son of Sir John Monson (of the Nicholas Stone tomb) who was created a baronet in 1611 (among the very first to be created); the third Baronet was created Lord Monson in 1728. There have been many interesting and gifted members of the family, prominent in Parliament, in the services (including an Elizabethan admiral) and the service of the Crown, but the fifth Lord was quite different. Anybody who knows Gatton Church in Surrey, standing in Capability Brown's park close to its great house, will recall its medieval exterior, of no special interest, and its interior filled to bursting with an incredible wealth of continental furnishings and stained glass. It is a breathtaking interior, dominated by late seventeenth-century Baroque canopied stalls, all arranged as in a college chapel – pulpit, altar, altar rails and so on – all richly carved. The hatchment (1841) of a Lincolnshire peer gives the clue: this interior is all the work of the fifth Lord Monson (1809–1841), who filled a very short life travelling and collecting. He was also a deeply religious man. Gatton church is his memorial; there is no memorial to him in Lincolnshire.

Gatton was only briefly a Monson house. It is, incidentally, of interest for another reason; it was perhaps the most rotten of all rotten boroughs. Until 1832 it returned two Members to Parliament. The 'Town Hall' is a small but elegant Doric garden temple (1765) close to the house, where elections were held and the handful of votes counted. Here stands a magnificent stone urn, inscribed 'Stat ductis sortibus urna'; 'After the lots have been drawn, the urn remains'.

All interested in local history owe a special debt of gratitude to the sixth Lord Monson, nineteenth-century antiquary and church-crawler, author of the famous *Church Notes*, which he wrote between 1828 and 1840, recording much that was swept away soon afterwards in the Victorian restorations all over the county.

Canwick is an austere early nineteenth-century house in a wonderful position. The Sibthorps were a talented and interesting family, who came here originally from Nottinghamshire in the early eighteenth century. Humphry Sibthorp was Sherardian Professor of Botany at Oxford, and Fellow of Magdalen. His younger son John succeeded him in the Oxford professorship and founded the Chair of Rural Economy. He was author of *Flora Oxoniensis* and other botanical works.

It was his nephew, Colonel Charles Sibthorp, an arch-Tory and Member of Parliament, who opposed the Reform Bill and Catholic Emancipation. When a Modern History

Society was established at Lancing College in the 1960s, it was named The Sibthorp Society in honour of Colonel Sibthorp. The founder, William Powell, then at the school, is now Conservative Member of Parliament for Corby (Northamptonshire).

Colonel Sibthorp's brother was the Reverend Richard Sibthorp, Fellow of Magdalen and Doctor of Divinity. Onetime an Anglican, he held various livings before being received into the Roman Catholic Church (1841). He was re-ordained, but two years later reverted to the Church of England, only to be readmitted to the Church of Rome in 1865. He died in 1879, but was buried, at his express wish, according to the rites of the Church of England. He founded St Anne's Bede Houses in Lincoln (1847), designed by Pugin (the Chapel by Butterfield). It is a pleasure to turn in here, and meditate on its remarkable founder.

The Sibthorp family is now extinct, and the house now flats. But its wonderful view of Lincoln Cathedral remains as wonderful as ever.

# XVIII

## Lincolnshire Houses
## and their Families: Kesteven

Travelling south along the Lincoln–Grantham road (A607), first comes Harmston, with its handsome early-Georgian front, dated 'G.T. 1710' (for Sir George Thorold, first Baronet of Harmston, later Lord Mayor of London, 1720). The Thorolds of Harmston descended from a second son of William Thorold of Marston (died 1569). The last Baronet of Harmston, Sir Nathaniel, was overwhelmed by his unexpected inheritance, and ran through his new fortune, so, deeply in debt, was obliged to go abroad. He left for Italy, and Harmston was locked up for years. He left in a hurry, because, when the house was eventually re-opened, it was discovered that the breakfast was still on the table, the chairs obviously hastily pushed aside and thrown over. The story is told in *Lord Halifax's Ghost Stories* Vol. II (Geoffrey Bles, 1937).

But Nathaniel emerged triumphant, first in Leghorn, then in Naples. With the help of a Neapolitan Jewish friend, he invented salted cod, a godsend for the Catholic population of Italy, who were thus enabled to observe their Friday abstinence. Nathaniel made a great new fortune, and built the Palazzo Inglese on Capri, where (as the family history puts it) 'he lived with a beautiful girl of Capri'. Unfortunately, she was already the wife of a Signor Antonio Canale; but they all lived happily together in the palazzo, and the Signor seemed happy to give his name to the Baronet's children. But there was of course, scandal locally, and the Bishop of Capri referred to the matter in his report to the Pope, *ad limina Apostollorum*, in 1754, stating that scandal had been caused 'by the cohabitation for many years, of a certain married woman with an heretical English noble-man'. However, his Holiness declined to be drawn into this. Nathaniel died in 1764 and his son Samuel, to whom his father had left his English property, came to Harmston to inherit. He arrived as Samuel Canale, but soon blossomed as Samuel Thorold, assuming his father's name and arms. He married the daughter of a Yorkshire parson-baronet at the age of twenty-one, and became High Sheriff of Lincoln-shire at twenty-five; not bad going for an illegitimate half-Italian. Alas, after various misfortunes, the line died out in the late nineteenth century, and the house was, until recently, a mental hospital.

Next door, Coleby Hall has had a rather less dramatic history. It is a charming, many-gabled house of 1628, like Harmston in a fine position overlooking the escarpment. It was built by the Lister family, and descended in the eighteenth century to Thomas Scrope (of the great Yorkshire family). He was himself an enthusiastic amateur of architecture, and a friend of Sir William Chambers, who built for him the most accomplished Temple of Romulus and Remus in the grounds (1762); Scrope himself designed a smaller temple in honour of Pitt in the garden. Coleby passed by marriage to the Tempests of Broughton in Yorkshire – an ancient and eminent Catholic family – who turned the Temple of Romulus and Remus into a Catholic Chapel, an unexpected use for a building dedicated to those heroes.

Close to the Nottinghamshire border is Doddington, one of the most important houses in the county. It was built at the very end of the sixteenth century by Thomas Tailor, Registrar to the Bishop of Lincoln, who made a great fortune out of land and the law; the architect was almost certainly the great Robert Smythson. It is always a thrill to approach the gabled gatehouse, with the great house standing behind, to walk through the gateway and come face to face with this towering late-Elizabethan front, glowing, like the gatehouse, with radiant old red brick. Its setting within its spacious walled garden is superb. It is a delightful surprise (perhaps) to find an eighteenth-century interior, with lofty, light, well proportioned Georgian rooms, white hall, parlour (a rather earlier eighteenth-century panelled interior) – and so up the grand eighteenth-century staircase to the drawing-room and state bedrooms on the first floor, the long gallery on the top. All this Georgian work was designed (for Sir John Hussey Delaval) by Thomas Lumby of Lincoln (*circa* 1761). Every room is a delight, not only the grand state rooms, but the smaller rooms too, such as the Holly bedroom with its tapestries and Gothick chimneypiece.

Doddington passed by marriage to the Husseys of Honington, and so to the legendary Delavals of Northumberland, albeit playing second fiddle (inevitably) to Seaton Delaval. It was Sarah, daughter and heiress of Edward Hussey Delaval, and wife of Captain Gunman, who bequeathed Doddington to Colonel G. R. T. Jarvis in 1829. It is his descendants who live here today, and open the place to the public. Concerts are regularly held in the Long Gallery, and there is a wonderful garden.

Not far away is Aubourn, which, like Doddington, stands immensely tall, a towering façade of old red brick; indeed it seems related to Doddington, and is perhaps the work of John Smythson (son of Robert). It is L-shaped with mullioned windows, stately, and yet at the same time homely, with front door and windows not quite symmetrically placed, and roof hipped and pantiled, perhaps an alteration in the next century, and perhaps replacing a flat lead roof and parapet. It is an altogether lovable house, partly a rebuilding of an earlier (sixteenth-century) house. It was built (or rebuilt) by Sir John Meres in the early seventeenth century; his wife was a Nevile, and in 1628 he sold it to his brother-in-law George Nevile. It has belonged to the Neviles ever since, though in the eighteenth century the family lived principally at Wellingore, their grander Georgian house (now flats or offices). Inside, there are delightful rooms with Jacobean panelling, and a spectacular early seventeenth-century staircase, with lavish strapwork panels and richly carved finials – altogether a triumph. Aubourn is now the home of Sir Henry Nevile K.C.V.O, who was until recently Lord Lieutenant of Lincolnshire.

Leadenham House is the grand late eighteenth-century home of the Reeves, a distinguished military family, who have for generations served in the Grenadier Guards; General John Reeve was one of Wellington's generals. It is a pleasure, on a summer evening, to drive along the lane near Stragglethorpe Church, and look towards the Cliff, with Leadenham House half-way up the hill, the tall church spire at its side, all lit up by the setting sun. The house was designed by Christopher Staveley of Melton Mowbray (1792–6); it is a building of fine proportions, with a restrained, reticent façade, standing erect against the tree-hung hill. Vulliamy made tactful additions in the early nineteenth century, and Detmar Blow's hand may be detected in the early twentieth-century decorations inside.

Following the construction of the new by-pass road round the edge of the park (1995), the present squire has courageously made a new drive up the hillside to the front door – a scheme which may have been envisaged when the house was built, for the avenue was planted, but no drive ever built. It is a great success. Leadenham commands wonderful views; towards Belvoir to the south, and across the Vale of Trent to the west, to the distant hills of Derbyshire on a clear day.

Fulbeck, next door, is quite different. The great pleasure here is to turn off the main road (A607) and drive through the early eighteenth-century wrought iron gates, recently gorgeously repaired and regilded, and up the avenue of tall ancient limes to the front door. The façade of the house is dated 1733 and may be compared with one of those distinguished early eighteenth-century houses in Stamford: there are giant Doric pilasters, and prominent keystones and 'Gibbs surrounds' to the windows. Inside, the hall and staircase are distinguished work; the dining-room (to the north) a slightly later, handsome addition. The gardens were laid out along the terrace to the north early this century by the Edwardian garden designer, Mr Innes Stuckey. Sir Francis Fane (younger son of the first Earl of Westmorland) first came to Fulbeck in 1632; the family are still here, and regularly open house and garden to the public.

Belton stands in the lush valley of the River Witham, north of Grantham, surrounded by a lovely and extensive park, watered by the river. The house was built by Sir John Brownlow between 1685 and 1689, and is perhaps the most celebrated late seventeenth-century house in England, serenely beautiful outside, and perfect with its sumptuous plasterwork and wood carvings within. Its architect is not known, but it could have been William Winde, who often employed William Stanton as mason-contractor, and Stanton was mason here. There is plasterwork by Edward Goudge and others, woodwork (perhaps) by Grinling Gibbons, and certainly by Edward Cartwright. Perhaps the most memorable rooms are the saloon, the chapel drawing-room, and the chapel itself. James Wyatt's library (1782) is certainly his great contribution to Belton. An ancient avenue of limes leads up from the east front to the Belmount Tower (known affectionately as 'Lord Brownlow's Trousers'); there are grand views from here across the park and surrounding countryside.

The Brownlows died out in the male line in the eighteenth century; their heiress married Sir John Cust, Speaker of the House of Commons, and their son was created Lord Brownlow, so the line and name have continued. In 1984 the present Lord Brownlow gave the house to the National

Trust (reserving a flat for his family). The whole place is magnificently maintained; house and gardens and park are regularly open to the public.

A few miles to the east is Culverthorpe, a captivating late seventeenth- early eighteenth-century house, little known to the outside world. It stands solitary on gently rising ground overlooking a long sheet of water and the wide undulating landscape beyond. It has something of the air of a French château, with its tall central block, with steeply pitched roof and tall chimneys, and was built *circa* 1680 for Sir John Newton (kinsman of Sir Isaac Newton). On either side are lower wings, each with a grand Venetian window, to light drawing-room and dining-room. These are the perfect foil for the central block, and may be the work of Roger Morris, the Palladian architect, who is known to have designed the London house for Sir Michael Newton. From these lower wings colonnades were planned – which actually appear in Badeslade's *View*, but were probably never built – though on either side we can see the first columns standing ready, attached to the house; they have waited patiently for 250 years, all in vain.

The family succession is complicated and rather odd. John Newton of Culverthorpe succeeded to the baronetcy of Newton of Barr's Court, Gloucestershire, who were namesakes but not in fact related. His grandson was Sir Michael, who built the wings. He married Lady Margaret Coningsby, daughter and heiress of the Earl of Coningsby, of Hampton Court, Herefordshire. She was created Countess of Coningsby in her own right, and Sir Michael and she had a son, John, Viscount Coningsby (1732). Alas, the family's pet monkey snatched the baby from his cradle, carried him up to the roof and dropped him over the parapet. The pathetic little marble slab to his memory lies in the floor of the Newton Chapel in Heydour Church, at the feet of his parents, the last Countess of Coningsby (1761) by Rysbrack, and Sir Michael Newton by Scheemakers (1743).

Heydour Church is a remarkable gallery of monuments to the family, by the best sculptors of the day.

Culverthorpe descended sideways to the family of Archer-Houblon, descendants of Sir John Houblon, first Governor of the Bank of England, whose head appeared recently on the £50 note (the name is pronounced Hublon). As they already possessed two other seats, Culverthorpe was often let, and finally sold (early in this century). It has passed through various hands recently; but this fascinating surprise house survives.

Of the other great palaces near Grantham, Harlaxton has already been described in Chapter VIII. Burn was employed here (in succession to Salvin); he was much employed in Lincolnshire at this time: at Revesby, for instance (see Chapter XI), and, nearer to Harlaxton, at Rauceby (1843), another characteristic house, built on a somewhat smaller scale, for the Willson family, the Sleaford bankers. In 1841 Burn was also at hand, and was commissioned by Christopher Turnor to rebuild at Stoke. The Turnors came here from Bedfordshire in the seventeenth century – and there was a seventeenth-century house first – then a Georgian mansion. A new and grander house, on a new site was required, and Burn provided this, in his familiar Elizabethan style.

The setting is delightful; approaching the house there appear on either side of the lake what appear to be grand pieces of theatrical scenery. They are in fact the arched entrances to the earlier stables (1676), set up here as enormous garden ornaments. They are most effective. The drive goes on, then turns at right angles to approach the house; here stands a sixty-foot obelisk to the honour of Newton, born at Woolsthorpe nearby. Stoke is a very grand house, and has something in common with Harlaxton, though Harlaxton is grander still and reflects the exotic tastes of Gregory Gregory. Christopher Turnor's tastes were more sober. Both are institutions now, Stoke being the headquarters of the National Union of Teachers.

Little Ponton, nearby, is now the seat of the Turnor family. This charming house belonged originally to a recusant branch of the Thorolds, and was a well known hide-out for Roman Catholic priests. There is in the overmantel in the Burston Room at Marston what is almost certainly a later seventeenth-century painting of Little Ponton; a square, seventeenth-century house, with hipped roof and dormers, crowned with tall chimneys, rather like a smaller version of Ashdown House in Berkshire, set in formal walled gardens. On the extinction of this branch of the family (1725), the place passed through various hands, before being acquired by the Turnors. In the past two centuries additions have been made to the seventeenth-century house, all in harmony; the seventeenth-century formal garden in the picture has been landscaped and is still very beautiful.

Irnham always delights, and is seemingly remote and withdrawn, the whole village unspoiled. Moreover, until the last corner is turned the house is invisible; then it appears, long, romantic L-shaped, early-Tudor – quite unlike any other house in the county. Apart from some damage in a fire in 1887 (which resulted in the rebuilding of the great hall and part of the north wing), it appears wonderfully untouched. The reason for its feeling of detachment is that until its sale in 1858 Irnham remained in Catholic hands, always descending sideways through old Catholic families – Thimelbys, Conquests and Arundells – distinguished families, but perhaps not in a position to rebuild in fashionable Georgian style. Thus the Tudor house has survived to give us pleasure today. In 1858, after the sale, a crucifix and paliasse bed were discovered in the priest's hiding place; all through the penal times, Mass had been said in the attic, and two Catholic priests are buried in the church:

†To the memory of the Reverend Mr Henry Brent, many years Chaplain to Lord and Lady Arundell . . . January 1787 . . . Requiescat in pace.

†To the memory of the Reverend Thomas Walton, Chaplain to Lord and Lady Arundell at Irnham ... 1797. Requiescat in pace.

Even the language of the inscriptions is distinctly Roman. Burial of Roman Catholics in the Anglican parish church was fraught with difficulties in the eighteenth century; such a service would usually take place at night, the rector in bed, or at any rate turning a blind eye.

For the past century or so Irnham has been in good Anglican hands, in the family of Woodhouse, and now of Benton-Jones, Baronets. It remains wonderfully unspoiled.

Casewick (pronounced Cassick) is also remote, in its ancient park near Stamford and remarkable with its courtyard, old buildings and walled enclosures and gardens. The house is part Jacobean, part eighteenth-century Gothick. The earlier south wing was built in 1621 by Thomas Trollope, soon after the family first came here. The family were Royalists and received a baronetcy from Charles I in 1642. The fourth Baronet *circa* 1785 commissioned William Legg of Stamford to add to this, and to him is due the gorgeous long west front in the most elegant Gothick taste, with gables and pinnacles and fanciful sugary crenellations, sash windows with Gothick glazing bars, and an ogee tripartite window to adorn the centre. An ancient wistaria flows across the entire front. Anthony Trollope the novelist. was great grandson of the fourth Baronet. The house is now flats, but much of the estate belongs to the family.

In Uffington nearby, the most handsome gates to the church were erected by the Honourable Charles Bertie, second son of the second Earl of Lindsey in 1679, and the yet more splendid gates opposite, with magnificent piers, crowned with urns, lead to a garden walk of the house. This is still kept up, though the house was destroyed by fire in 1904, and never rebuilt. There are also grand gates and lodges to the east, where the road twists and turns towards Market Deeping. These two gateways are now being restored. Uffington still belongs to the family, the agent's house now used as the residence.

Grimsthorpe is Lincolnshire's greatest and grandest seat. It is a pleasure to drive along the road (from Corby Glen to Edenham) which borders the park; first there is the glimpse of Capability's lake (where the lane to Swinstead turns off), then the view, down the wide north avenue, to the north front – Vanbrugh's north front, unmistakably Vanbrugh's, even at this distance; then, at the turn into the village, the great presence of the castle makes itself felt above us, Vanbrugh's towers, the Riding School; from then on we can observe the castle unfold itself, the whole east front with its grand windows lighting the state rooms, then King John's Tower, and so round to the many-gabled south front. The delight of Grimsthorpe is that it combines the intimate charms of the medieval and Tudor castle, with the magnificence of Vanbrugh's grand north front.

King John's Tower, of course, is the original castle; this and Vaudey Abbey (Vallis Dei), the Cistercian foundation (1147) on the far side of the lake, would have dominated the scene in 1516 when Henry VIII granted Grimsthorpe to the tenth Lord Willoughby de Eresby. It had been built in the early thirteenth century by Gilbert de Gant, Earl of Lincoln. Lord Willoughby would then have been seated at Eresby (see p. 95), and his daughter married Charles Brandon, Duke of Suffolk, and it was he and his wife who built the quadrangular castle (which still exists) on to King John's Tower, to receive the King in 1541.

The Duke of Suffolk was thirty years older than his wife, and their two children died young. After his death she married Richard Bertie (pronounced Bartie) 'the fortunate gentleman from Sussex who wooed and won the heiress of the Willoughbys, the Duchess of Suffolk'. The family descend from their son who became the twelfth Lord Willoughby de Eresby.

'The trouble with our family, Henry, is that we're always dying out,' the late Lord Ancaster once remarked to the author. All too true. The Berties became Earls of Lindsey, and Dukes of Ancaster. There were five Dukes, but then the title became extinct. The ancient barony of Willoughby de Eresby (which can descend through the female line) then went (by marriage) to the Burrells, Lords Gwydyr, but after one more generation that title died out. The next Baroness married Sir Gilbert Heathcote, Baronet of Normanton, Rutland, and the Heathcotes became Barons Aveland, and Earls of Ancaster; but now these titles, for want of an heir male, have become extinct. On the death of the third Earl, in 1983, his daughter became Baroness Willoughby de Eresby, the twenty-seventh holder of that historic title. She is the present châtelaine of Grimsthorpe.

For anybody visiting the castle there is a feast of pleasure. Next to the Vanbrugh Hall, Vanbrugh's most dramatic interior, is the Chapel, with its elaborate stucco decoration, probably designed by Hawksmoor, after Vanbrugh's death (1726); the State Drawing-Rooms are breathtaking, and there is any amount of pleasure to be found in the smaller family rooms on the south and west sides of the Tudor courtyard – if, indeed, we are invited in.

But, above all, it is the scale of everything which makes Grimsthorpe utterly wonderful. Grimsthorpe is in scale with the great rolling country of grass and corn, just as a château like Oiron is in scale with the extensive central French countryside. As Christopher Hussey has said, 'Like Lory in *The Relapse*, standing before the mighty façade, we expect to have the giant come out, by and by, with his club.'

# XIX

# The Royal Air Force in Lincolnshire

Lincolnshire is sometimes referred to as the home of the Royal Air Force; indeed wherever we go in Lincolnshire, but especially in Kesteven and Lindsey, there are things to remind us of the R.A.F. The wide open spaces, the sparse population, the empty countryside, the absence of industrial haze all combine to make the county ideal for flying. In 1945 there were in all some eighty R.A.F. bases in Lincolnshire. Most of them are now but a memory, but in many of them there are odd, unexpected reminders of wartime flying which will continue to be of interest in days to come.

Go to South Carlton and visit the church. There is a somewhat unusual rectangular pulpit, which proves to be a memorial to the men of the Royal Flying Corps who served at the South Carlton airfield during the Great War. South Carlton, on the edge of the escarpment, on the edge of high ground, was an ideal site; the prevailing south-west wind assisted the aeroplanes in their take off. But South Carlton airfield began life in 1916 merely as a relief landing ground; the early aeroplanes had only a limited range, and these relief landing grounds would be manned by a single airman, armed only with a telephone, who would be billeted in a local farmhouse, and the farmer would receive only a 'retainer' to keep fields under grass, and to remove all livestock in times of need. There were relief landing Grounds at Brattleby, Gainsborough, Kirton-in-Lindsey, Elsham and so on. Brattleby, renamed, developed into the celebrated Scampton R.A.F. Station. But in these early days it was mainly a matter of home defence against the Zeppelin.

There was still something amateurish, too, in those early days, about flying methods and even about those early 'flying machines', which were somewhat brittle affairs. There is the story of that amusing incident when an early 'plane', having a little difficulty in landing, collided with a cow. The machine was a complete 'write-off', but the only damage to the cow was the loss of a horn, which was duly mounted on a shield, and is preserved at the Museum at Old Warden in Bedfordshire.

In 1918 South Carlton developed into Number 46 Training Squadron, but all was disbanded at the end of the war, and only a few minor buildings survive on the high ground, together with the pulpit in the church to remind us of those days. In the early 1930s, with the rise of Hitler, there came the call for rearmament. This led to the re-establishment of airfields, and the construction of new and much larger R.A.F. stations, such as Scampton, Waddington and Binbrook, for Bomber Command. Coningsby and East Kirkby were established in the early 1940s.

It was in 1914 that Cranwell was chosen as a site for HMS *Daedalus*, the R.N.A.S. training station, which was ideal in its situation and landscape, being on high, open ground, in proximity to coastal bombing and gunnery ranges. By 1918 the camp covered about three thousand acres; it was in this year that the R.N.A.S. and the Royal Flying Corps merged, to form the R.A.F.

The magnificent buildings date from 1931; the college had previously been housed in huts. Sir Samuel Hoare was then Secretary of State for Air; he was also Member of Parliament for the London borough of Chelsea. It was he who suggested to the architect, Sir James Grey West, that something on the lines of Chelsea Hospital might be appropriate. The buildings in red brick, dressed with stone, planned with great lawns, plantations, avenues and vistas, are like a twentieth-century version of Chelsea. The Chapel, like a Wren City church, is an excellent addition of 1962. There is a most interesting museum, on the road up to North Rauceby, housed in old farm buildings.

Moving into the realms of the Second World War, we ought to visit The Lion and Royal at Navenby. An old brass plate will inform us that the suffix 'Royal' was added by command of H.R.H. the Prince of Wales (later Edward VII), to commemorate the fact that on 3 March 1887 he changed his clothes in an upstairs room after hunting with Mr Chaplin's hounds nearby (i.e. Mr Henry Chaplin of Blankney). A front room downstairs is named the Guy Gibson Room. This is to celebrate the fact that Wing-Commander Guy Gibson, VC DSO and bar, spent two years here, with his wife, 1942–4, when serving with 617 Squadron – 'the Dambusters'.

Wellingore village lies on the main road to Lincoln, along the Cliff; the original Roman road (Ermine Street) runs behind. Here we shall find the relics of R.A.F. Wellingore. There is a grand, long, flat field not far from the edge of the Cliff, and a few odd buildings survive. Ermine Street at this point becomes a green lane, and here stands an iron plaque marked 'Former R.A.F. Wellingore'. A moving reminder.

Not so many miles away is Woodhall Spa. Here we can make for the celebrated Petwood Hotel, and we shall find that it is flying the flag of the R.A.F. This is a special privilege granted to the hotel to commemorate its use as Officers' Mess, 617 Squadron in 1943 and 1944 at the time of the incredible bombing of the Mohne and Eder Dams in Germany. The raid took place on 16 May 1943. The day before, Guy Gibson's beloved dog Nigger was run over, and he left instructions that Nigger should be buried at R.A.F. Scampton at the precise time that the raid on the dams was to take place. And so it was. In the Guy Gibson Room at The Lion and Royal there are many photographs of the man, his friends and his planes – and of Nigger. There are more, too, at Petwood, and opposite the front door of the hotel, in a flower bed, is a rusty and somewhat deformed lump of iron. A notice nearby reads 'One of the only remaining proto-types of the famous Barnes Wallis Bouncing Bomb'.

Some way from here, high on the Lincolnshire Wolds, not far from Louth, is Kelstern. There is no village proper – only a collection of cottages, the church and Kelstern Hall. But high on top of the Wolds nearby can still be seen the runways of the wartime airfield. Bruce Barrymore Half-penny, writing in *Action Stations* Vol. II (published by Patrick Stephens Ltd) remarks: 'Kelstern has a strange, silent atmosphere, which you feel as you stand on the wartime main runway. It is not possible to kill the airfield by taking down the huts, and as the mists begin to roll in, you cannot help but wonder what the tired crews thought as they returned from their missions to such airfields as this.' At a remote road junction nearby, a small monument has been erected to the memory of those members of 625 Squadron who did not return to base. This is a last remaining link with those wartime days; it is a link of which Lincolnshire may be proud.

# XX

# A Great Agriculturalist

Lincolnshire, as we all know, is a great agricultural county, and the finest soil of all is in the fens. Kirton-in-Holland is one of the largest of all the fen villages, with a mammoth and wonderful church, a few attractive Georgian houses, a busy main street (the main A16 road running through) and a number of public houses. Just off the main street, to the south, stands the town hall, an unusual brick building, designed by Henry Kidd, a local architect, erected in 1911 to celebrate George V's coronation; it has an almost French-looking tower, crowned with an iron corona. In front of this is a statue, cast in bronze, by Philip Lindsey Clark (1930) of a seated figure, erect and commanding. Beneath, in the base of Portland stone, are carved panels; one shows a grave of potatoes, with a fork and a riddle, and in front the words: WILLIAM DENNIS 1841–1924. William Dennis is an almost legendary figure. The story runs that he arrived in Kirton in 1861, with his scythe, his sickle and his gathering rake slung over his back, sat down on a milestone outside the church, and that he died a millionaire.

The legend is true. William Dennis was born in 1841, in Horsington (between Horncastle and Woodhall Spa), the son of a farm foreman. At the age of twenty he set off to walk to Kirton, some twenty miles distant (everybody then travelled on foot, if they could not afford a horse), to seek his fortune. He arrived outside the church, sat down on a milestone, and spun a coin; should he stay in Kirton? or should he move on? It was heads for Kirton, tails for moving on. It was heads.

Soon a local farmer passed by and seeing him sitting on the milestone, said, 'You look as if you need some work?' So he offered him work on his nearby farm. As soon as he arrived in Kirton, William realised that the rich silt of the area was ideal for growing potatoes. Potatoes it was to be.

William Dennis was intelligent, thrifty, hard-working, and determined, but above all, he was an honourable God-fearing man, a devout Methodist. He took lodgings nearby, and three years later, on 28 June 1864, he married Sarah Ann Whitworth in the church of St Peter and St Paul, Algarkirk, the next parish. She was six months younger than he, and they were married for over fifty-six years. She (with five sons and four daughters) was his life-long support.

William always said that the first £1,000 took the most saving; and it was in 1871 that he made his first land purchase of six acres in the parish of Kirton, and on this he built himself a house and for the first time began farming on his own account.

As time went by, his five sons went into partnership with him. His potato enterprise continued to grow – so did his fortune. He bought more and more land during the years of agricultural depression, towards the end of the century, and as nearby farms became available, he bought them and revived them. At one time he and his sons farmed and owned 20,000 acres – much of it in Lincolnshire, but some in Cambridgeshire and Huntingdonshire – some as far away as Sussex. He was a man of great enterprise, building light railway systems to serve many of his farms and installing his own private telephone service which connected the farms to his Head Office in Kirton.

By 1914 he and his sons had made their fortune.

All his sons were men of ability too. John, the eldest, took charge of the business in London and New York, and became Mayor of Westminster and Member of Parliament for a Birmingham seat. He was Potato Controller in the

Ministry of Food in Whitehall in the Great War, and was often nicknamed 'Mr Covent Garden'. Joseph, the second son, worked with his elder brother in London, and in Jersey, St Malo, and elsewhere in Europe; he was a great sportsman and keen racing man. Herbert, the third brother, worked for the firm in South Lincolnshire, and was a dedicated countryman, a keen shooting and hunting man. He lived at Nocton Hall (built by Lord Gooderich, later Earl of Ripon, a former Prime Minister) for some years. Thomas, the fourth brother, a brilliant linguist, travelled widely in the service of the potato, and was for many years Chairman of the *Lincolnshire Standard* newspaper.

Frank, the youngest son, like his elder brother Herbert, bought a country house, that fascinating and romantic eighteenth-century seat of the Tunnards and Tunnards-Moores – Frampton Hall – in the next village to Kirton. From here he was able to administer the great enterprises nearby, and as the longest-lived of the brothers became the doyen of this generation.

So the great Dennis kingdom grew and flourished; in 1906 William became a Justice of the Peace and, in due time, Chairman of the Holland County Council. He was widely travelled, having visited (often in the service of the potato) the United States of America and Canada, Egypt and the Canary Islands, and much of Europe. It was not for nothing that he was widely known as the 'Potato King'. In 1917/18 as the scourge of the German U-boat grew, stocks of food in the country became very low. In the month of May 1917, for instance, German U-Boats had sunk 526,447 tons of British and Allied shipping, and during the same month a further 340,163 tons of neutral shipping, much of which was bringing food and supplies to this country. With no more than two weeks' supply of food in the country, Lord Milner – a member of Lloyd George's War Cabinet – appealed, with tears of emotion in his eyes, to arable farmers (particularly to those in the fertile fens) to plant and grow yet more acres of potatoes. This they did, thus helping to save the country in its hour of need.

At home, William Dennis was a generous employer, as were his sons. Sometimes parties of their employees were taken for a day's outing to London, by special train from Kirton station (on the old East Lincolnshire Railway), followed by a great dinner party at some famous London restaurant. There were parties, too, at home, with a sit-down dinner in their large warehouse, decorated for the occasion with flags and bunting. It was William who built Kirton town hall, and largely financed the building of the Methodist Church. Too little has been written about him; this is a chance to redress the balance.

William Dennis's great farming empire continues to flourish under his grandson and great grandsons, and the former, Mr Peter Dennis of Stenigot, was High Sheriff of the County a few years ago.

The story is told that on one of his sea voyages William Dennis stood on deck scanning the horizon, surveying the ocean, deep in thought.

'What are you thinking about?' he was asked.

'I was thinking if only the sea were land. What a wonderful farm it would be.'

We salute William Dennis, great son of Lincolnshire, and founder of a wonderful agricultural empire.

# Epilogue

During the months in which these pages have been written, news has come – more than welcome news – that the liberation of northern Lincolnshire is at hand, that the hated 'Humberside' (so-called) will be no more. It is hard to conceive how any government in its senses could have created such a monstrosity, against the wishes of the electorate. When the idea was first proposed, a poll was taken in northern Lindsey: Do you wish to remain Lincolnshire, or would you prefer to form part of a new county of 'Humberside'? Ninety-seven per cent voted to remain in Lincolnshire. This vote was totally ignored by Mr Heath's government; the so-called 'Humberside' was created, which included Grimsby and Cleethorpes, Barton-on-Humber and Brigg, Scunthorpe and the countryside around. It also included a larger section of the East Riding of Yorkshire. 'Humberside' indeed! The very name is distasteful. It provided a fitting epitaph for Mr Heath's government (1974).

Mr Auberon Waugh, writing some months later in the *Spectator* or the *Daily Telegraph*, spoke of a visit he had lately paid to so-called 'Humberside', and expressed surprise that apparently no statues of Mr Heath and Mr Peter Walker had been erected in the market places of Grimsby, Brigg and Scunthorpe. 'Humberside' was unpopular from the start, and every effort to popularise it, of course, failed. 'Welcome to England's newest County HUMBERSIDE' proclaimed the county signs. That banal word 'welcome', too! All efforts to make the authorities think again were of no avail. 'Humberside' signs at the

133

frontiers were torn down or mutilated; the name was deeply resented. The author can claim with pride and pleasure that he never put 'Humberside' on any envelope, and that his two Lincolnshire books, published in 1976 and 1989, simply made no reference to 'Humberside', even on a map: it was entirely ignored. Yorkshire, too, had its own ways of ignoring the loathsome word. 'I am told', the squire of Scawby (Colonel R. Sutton-Nelthorpe) said to the author as early as 1976, 'that if we push hard enough, we can chase the enemy out.'

At the same time, we can rejoice with Rutland, our next-door and greatly loved county, which is to regain its independence soon after ours. For a long time, in recent years, the 'planners' and 'do-gooders', the busy bodies and interferers, have longed to destroy that most beautiful county of Rutland. There was an attempt in the early 1960s, when Mr Macmillan was Prime Minister. Every time we crossed the frontier, we were greeted by those provocative signs (rightly provocative) 'Rutland fights to keep local government local'. They were victorious. *The Times* – blessed in those days in having no front page news – put the principal news in the middle pages, and only a single column at that (except on occasions of special importance). In August 1964, on the middle pages, as the principal column on the left proclaimed 'Independence for Malta', the one on the right announced 'Independence for Rutland'. The signpost on the Great North Road was changed to 'Rutland keeps local Government local'.

But of course the 'planners' and 'do-gooders', the moralising interferers, saw that they had another chance coming to destroy a county which had so defied them. But once again, by keeping their 'Rutland' signs up at the frontiers (encouraged by Leicestershire), and by refusing to write 'Leicestershire' on their letters, the county of Rutland has won through. But why have we to go through all this nonsense? And who pays for it?

So here in Lincolnshire we salute those who have stood firm against the tyranny of Whitehall and so-called 'democracy'. Ill will to the creators of 'Avon', of 'Tyne and Wear', of 'Hereford and Worcester' (an absurd title); but, above all, ill wishes to the creators of 'Humberside'. 'Humberside', so-called, ceases to exist on 31 March 1996. How the bells will ring on both sides of the Humber!

# Bibliography

Barley, Maurice: *Lincolnshire and the Fens*, Batsford (1952)

Cox, Dr J. Charles: *Methuen's Little Guide* (1916)

Hill, Sir Francis: *Mediaeval Lincoln*; *Tudor and Stuart Lincoln*; *Georgian Lincoln*; *Victorian Lincoln*; Cambridge U.P. (1966)

Kelly's *Directory to Lincolnshire* (1933)

Mee, Arthur; *Lincolnshire* (The King's England), Hodder & Stoughton (1949)

Monson, 6th Lord: *Lincolnshire Church Notes* (1846), edited by 9th Lord Monson, Lincoln Record Society (1936)

*Murray's Handbook to Lincolnshire* (1890)

Pevsner, N., Harris, J. and Antram, N.: Lincolnshire (The Buildings of England) Penguin Books, second edition (1989)

Rawnsley, W. F.: *Highways and Byways in Lincolnshire*, Macmillan (1914)

Thorold, Henry: *Lincolnshire Churches Revisited*, Foreword by H.R.H. The Prince of Wales, Michael Russell, second edition (1993)

Thorold, Henry (ed.): *Lincolnshire Churches, their Past and their Future*, Lincolnshire Old Churches Trust (1976)

Thorold, Henry, and Yates, Jack: *Shell Guide to Lincolnshire*, Faber & Faber (1965)

Sympson, E. Mansel: *Memorials of Old Lincolnshire*, George Allen (1911)

*White's Directory of Lincolnshire* (1842)

# Index

Chaplin, Henry, 96, 127
Cholmeley, Sir Montague, 1st Baronet, 110
Christian, Ewan, 26
Clark, Philip Lindsey, 129
Claxby, 104
Clayton and Bell, 83
Cleethorpes, 39, 133
Cliff, the, 1, 6, 34, 56
Clinton and Saye, Edward, 9th Lord, 29
Coleby, 34
Coleby Hall, 115
Collins, William, 110
Comper, Sir Ninian, 66
Coningsby, 126
Coningsby, Countess of, 119
Copledyke, Thomas, 101
Corby Glen, 30
Cotes-by-Stow, 22, 89
Cotton, John, 67
Cox, J. Charles, 51–2
Cracroft family, 110
Cracroft-Eley, Mrs Robin, 111
Cranwell, 126–7
Croft, 91
Cromwell, Ralph, Lord, 8, 91
Crowle, 44
Crowther, J. S., 42
Croyland, 23–4
Culverthorpe, 119, 120
Curzon of Kedleston, Marquess, 8
Cust, Sir John, 118

Dashwood family, 104
Dashwood, Sir Francis, 56–7
De Wint, Peter, 57
Delaval family, 116
Dennis, Frank, 131
Dennis, Herbert, 131
Dennis, John, 130–31
Dennis, Joseph, 131
Dennis, Peter, 132
Dennis, Thomas, 131
Dennis, William, 129–32
Denton, 33, 97
Doddington, 19–20, 115–16
Donington, 24, 82
Dymoke family, 103
Dymoke, John, 103

Eadnoth II, Bishop of Dorchester, 22
Earle, Sir Richard, 3rd Baronet, 88
East Kirkby, 126
Easton, 97
Eastville, 81
Edenham, 12, 30, 65
Edward VI, 36
Edward VII, 127
Eginton, Francis, 107
Elizabeth I, Queen, 76
Elmhirst, Dorothy, 3
Elmhirst, Leonard, 2–3

Elmhirst, Richard, 2
Elsham, 45, 108–9, 125
Elst, Mrs van der, 33
Elwes, Geoffrey, 108, 109
Elwes, Gervase, 45
Elwes, Guy, 108, 109
Elwes, Jeremy, 109
Elwes, Lady Winefride, 45
Epworth, 43, 44
Eresby House, 12, 65, 95, 123
Ermine Street, 1, 29, 50, 58, 110

Fane, Sir Francis, 118
Fens, the, 1–2, 25
Fenton, 20
Fillingham Castle, 110
Firsby, 53, 54
Fleet, 24, 81
Folkingham, 30, 85
Fosdyke, 80
Fossdyke, the, 20, 50
Fossway, the, 50, 58
Foster, Peter, 33, 97
Fowler, James, 39, 63, 102
Fox, Richard, Bishop of Winchester, 33, 74
Frampton, 24, 82
Frampton Hall, 131
Franklin, Sir John, 64
Freiston, 49, 82
Friskney, 12, 47
Frithville, 81
Fulbeck, 34, 56, 85, 117–18

Gace, Joseph, 93
Gainsborough, 22, 71–2, 125
Gate Burton Hall, 19
Gautby, 90, 94
Gedney, 24, 55, 84
Gedney Drove End, 26
Gedney Dyke, 27
Gedney Hill, 24, 79
George III, King, 13
Gibbons, Grinling, 118
Gibraltar Point, 11
Gibson, Guy, 127
Gilbert of Sempringham, St, 28
Glenworth Hall, 95–6
Goderich, Viscount, *later* 1st Earl of
  Ripon, 87, 131
Gosberton, 82–3
Goudge, Edward, 118
Goxhill, 40
Grainger, Percy, 45
Grantham, 33, 52, 53, 62, 72–4, 97
Grantham, Thomas, 9–10
Great Hale, 29
Great Ponton, 33, 85
Great Steeping, 9
Green, Thomas, 88
Gregory, Gregory, 32, 120